Jewish Feminists

T0307870

Dina Pinsky JEWISH

FEMINISTS

Complex Identities and Activist Lives

UNIVERSITY OF ILLINOIS PRESS

Urbana and Chicago

© 2010 by the Board of Trustees
of the University of Illinois
All rights reserved
Manufactured in the United States of America
1 2 3 4 5 C P 5 4 3 2 1
♾ This book is printed on acid-free paper.

Library of Congress Cataloging-in-Publication Data
Pinsky, Dina.
Jewish feminists : complex identities and
activist lives / Dina Pinsky.
p.   cm.
Includes bibliographical references and index.
ISBN 978-0-252-03486-2 (cloth : alk. paper) —
ISBN 978-0-252-07677-0 (pbk. : alk. paper)
1. Feminists—United States.
2. Jews—Identity.
3. Feminism—Religious aspects—Judaism.
4. Feminism—United States.
I. Title.
HQ1421.P56   2010
296.082'0973—dc22   2009024501

Contents

Acknowledgments   vii

Introduction   1

CHAPTER 1   Torah Warriors   21

CHAPTER 2   Secular Adapters   43

CHAPTER 3   Encountering Difference   60

CHAPTER 4   Patriarchal Opposers   80

Conclusion   95

Appendix: Biographical Sketches   99

Notes   115

Index   131

Acknowledgments

There are many special people who helped me in the process of researching and writing this book. Any omission here is due to error rather than lack of gratitude.

I am very grateful to the Jewish feminists who made this work possible by sharing their life stories with me.

I am also indebted to the many friends and colleagues who offered suggestions and advice on the development of this project or read parts of this work at various stages of its progress. I am especially grateful to Laura Levitt and Barbara Katz Rothman for their generous and wise mentorship and advice. I would also like to express my appreciation to Patricia Clough, Hester Eisenstein, Charles Kadushin, Catherine Silver, Bob Alford, Cynthia Fuchs Epstein, Judith Lorber, and Susan Farrell. Thank you to Tania Levey for being a wonderful sounding board for my ideas; it was in a phone conversation with her that I first hit upon this topic. Jennifer Moore, a very dear long-time buddy, was always interested in reading chapters. I am also grateful to other friends who helped me with some of the more technical details included in this book: Jack Levinson, Susan Sapiro, Lewis Polishook, Dan Werlin, Rabbi Danya Ruttenberg, and Rabbi Sarah Rubin. And a special thank you to my cousin, Rabbi Hillel Norry, who is always willing to answer my sh'eilot.

Thank you to the members of my writing groups, in their various incarnations, for encouragement and useful feedback, and for providing me with deadlines: Melissa Ditmore, Jean Halley, Belkis Suazo-Garcia, Betsy Wissinger, Cristiane Carneiro, Jose Marrero, and Alex Otieno. I would also like to thank the members of the Philadelphia Jewish Feminist Scholars and Writers Group, who have played a role in the development of my thinking about Jewish feminist issues, especially Michelle Friedman, Lori Lefkowitz, Laura Levitt, and Miriam Peskowitz. I am especially grateful to Caryn Aviv and Rebecca Alpert for their thoughtful reviews of the manuscript. Thanks to Kendra Boileau, Cecelia Cancellaro, and Jane Lyle for their expert editorial work.

I want to thank my departmental colleagues for providing such a warm and hospitable working environment for me: Ana María García, Jonathan Church, John Noakes, Doreen Loury, Alex Otieno, Luca Follis, and Norman Johnston. I would like to gratefully acknowledge the support of the Arcadia University Faculty Development Fund. Thanks to two of my brightest students for their assistance with references and coding: Suzanne Hasty and Lauren Swartz.

Beyond those who directly helped me with this work are those who have indirectly helped through their all-around love and support. I am grateful for my family's love and loyalty: Alice and Terry Shapiro, David Pinsky, Mark Pinsky, and Melissa Pinsky. Katie and Dave Elsila have always shown interest in my work and provided intellectual encouragement. Thank you also to Jamie Elsila Cook, Kari Elsila, and their families. My most tireless reader and editor has been Mikael Elsila. I am extremely thankful for his generous supply of enthusiasm and for the energy he has devoted to my work and, more importantly, to our family. I am lucky to be the beneficiary of his embodiment of feminism in the way he partners with me in parenting and marriage. I do not take for granted how his choices about the way he lives his life (made possible by the feminist movement) have provided this mother with the time and energy to complete this book. The book is dedicated to our sons, Sol and Ilan, and to the hope that they will grow up in a world of increased activism and equality.

Jewish Feminists

Introduction

I first felt God when I was sixteen.

Up until then, I was a typical 1980s suburban American Jewish teenager. Having attended Jewish day school and then declared myself an atheist, I was undergoing a small, private rebellion. But then I visited Israel on a summer teen tour and had an unexpected religious awakening. To put it bluntly, the moment I saw the Western Wall, I began to believe in God.[1] I made up my mind to begin observing the Jewish dietary laws and Sabbath as soon as I returned home. (The rest of my trip was a different story. I was regularly chastised by my counselors for disobeying the rules of religious observance: "Dina, turn off the hairdryer! It's the Sabbath!")[2] I wanted to practice Judaism on my own terms in my own way. Thus I began a journey of idiosyncratic beliefs and practices that continues to this day.

After my Israel experience, I chose to transfer from my neighborhood public school to the only Jewish high school in town. This "yeshiva high school" was run by ultra-Orthodox rabbis.[3] Most of my classes were gender-segregated, and my Jewish subject classes were taught by bearded, black-hat-wearing rabbis. I made new friends in the Orthodox community who regularly invited me to stay at their houses for the Sabbath.

However, being in the Orthodox world did have some drawbacks for me. I had been raised in egalitarian Jewish settings. In my Conservative Jewish elementary school, youth group, and synagogue, I had always been asked to lead services and participate fully in ritual life.[4] In the Orthodox high school, I was not even allowed to learn Talmud (the compilation of oral law) because it was considered inappropriate for girls. And forget about leading services anymore. As is the Orthodox custom, males and females were separated by a physical divider in our school's morning services. I could not even see the proceedings in the boys' section. I quickly learned, to my surprise, that the role of females in traditional Judaism was to be silent observers of religious rituals. That shocked me.

Thus began my awareness of the need for feminism in the Jewish community. I did my part by routinely pestering my rabbinic teachers. They answered my questions about why girls could not learn Talmud with lame explanations about gender roles: "Girls do not need to learn the same things as boys because they will be doing different things when they grow up." (What they meant was: men are responsible for praying and studying Torah, and women are responsible for the family, cooking, and cleaning.) But they did concede that if I was determined to learn some Talmud, there were a few areas that might be acceptable to study: the parts about *kashrut* (Jewish dietary laws) and *niddah* (laws governing sex in marriage and menstrual customs).

This confused me. After all, I regularly asked my male friends what they had learned after they finished their daily double period of Talmud, and they would tell me that they had learned about different sexual positions or different kinds of nasal mucus. Those reports left me wondering how learning to translate Aramaic writing about the intricacies of bodily secretions would help prepare boys to be leaders in the Jewish world. And is this subject matter really too esoteric and advanced for girls' feeble minds?

So I asked the rabbis to teach me Talmud during my lunch break. I thought they would not be able to resist the aspirations of a student who was yearning so much to learn more intensively that she would sacrifice her only free time at school. I begged and pleaded, but they never acquiesced. The closest any of the rabbis came to agreeing was when Rabbi S. said that he might do it, but he would have to work off of a photocopied page from the text (that is, not the physical book itself), and we could not let his colleagues find out![5]

As I continued my journey in the Orthodox community during college, I continued to experience cognitive dissonance about my role as a woman in Judaism. I was getting to know young women with their sights set on top-notch careers who compartmentalized their backseat roles within Judaism. They planned to be investment bankers, law partners, and surgeons, but would not chant Torah in front of a congregation or even lead blessings at their family table.[6]

As my college education helped me think more critically and I became more entrenched in an Orthodox friendship network, I began to feel quite conflicted. I attended Orthodox services more than three times a week, where I was hidden behind a divider in the women's section. At the same time, I was becoming more interested in women's studies and progressive politics. For me, Judaism and feminism seemed to be a contradiction in terms. This tension actually became the basis for my senior thesis.

Fast-forward to graduate school, where I was in the middle of a Ph.D. in sociology. I had not abandoned my interest in Jewish feminist issues, yet I still framed that interest as a personal spiritual and religious project. In addition to my Ph.D., I decided to take on a certificate in women's studies. When reading for my classes, I was surprised to come across writings by second-wave feminists who said that being Jewish was a root cause for their feminism.[7] They viewed Jewish feminism differently than I did, framing it not in conflict but in coherence. I was so used to struggling to be a religiously practicing feminist that this idea was shocking to me. I had never realized that growing up Jewish could actually inspire someone to be a feminist in a positive way. This concept fascinated me and led to the desire to learn more about that generation of Jewish activists, which ultimately led to this book.

RESEARCHING THE SELF

Why is my story important? When researchers explain where they stand, readers can better evaluate the research. Knowing that kind of personal history helps readers uncover the extent of a researcher's insider's knowledge of a subject as well as any potential biases. Also, all life stories follow certain patterns. Later in this volume, I present my interviewees' identities as shifting, multiple, and often contradictory. And so, too, this brief account of my own personal history shows how, like all Jewish identities, mine has changed over time and has been created in complicated and often contradictory ways. This kind of ambivalent and complex way of negotiating identities is, in fact, what this book is all about.

This book is about making sense of what it means to be composed of varied and dynamic selves. It is a study in identity construction. More specifically, it is about Jewish feminist identities. In the following pages, you will be introduced to Jewish people who participated in the feminist movement of the 1970s. Using their stories about their lives, I explore the creative ways in which Jewish feminists make sense of their identities.

Yet this book is essentially also about what it means to identify strongly with different communities that often have contradictory demands. It is about what it means to be a member of a group, both individually and collectively. What it means to be Jewish is just as much a changing and complex concept as what it means to be feminist or American or liberal or even a woman. These identity categories are contested—they are defined differently even by people who call themselves by the same name.

Individual identities are formed by the web of community belongings and roles that we all occupy. As a sociologist, I am not as interested in individual people as I am in what groups of individuals have in common. The self is not created in a vacuum but is influenced by the surrounding society. More specifically, each person is a member of many different groups with different statuses and identities throughout life. Ideas about who we are come from our connections to these groups. Members of communities or cultures collectively construct the norms and beliefs of that group. "What it means to be a _____" is a changing concept that is defined differently in different contexts. For instance, what it meant to be a woman in 1950 is radically different from what it means today. Combine that complexity with the fact that we each are members of many different cultures at once, and you have a fascinatingly complex topic to explore.

The book is based on a research study I conducted in which I interviewed Jewish women and men who participated in the feminist movement of the 1960s and 1970s.[8] Of the thirty people discussed here (twenty-five women and five men), all identify as Jews and have two Jewish parents. However, the way in which they identify and practice (or do not practice) Judaism varies greatly. They all participated in some aspect of the feminist movement as well as in other movements of the time. Like their Jewish orientations, their activist experiences and identities are diverse. Both categories, Jewish and feminist, are contested and are seen as operating on a continuum. In other words, people often think of themselves or others as being "more" or "less" Jewish or feminist. By defining both categories according to self-identification, I ended up with a diverse group of research participants with respect to both variables—Jewish and feminist.

I interviewed people living in various regions of the United States, knowing that place of residence has an impact on identity.[9] I asked them to share with me their individual Jewish autobiographies and feminist autobiographies, and to discuss how the two fit together. These life history interviews resulted in rich data that reflects a lifetime of identity building. They combine with my analysis to tell a provocative story about the construction of social identities.

WHY IS THIS BOOK DIFFERENT FROM OTHER BOOKS?

Most students of feminism know that by the 1980s, women of color began asserting that the feminist conception of "woman" was not only monolithic but also exclusionary; it failed to acknowledge diversity among women.[10] Moreover, this definition of woman was based on the assumptions of white heterosexual middle-class women and thus reflected their own perspectives, omitting the experiences and everyday realities of women of color, lesbians, and non-middle-class women, among others.

Since then, feminist theorists have pondered the implications of exclusion in feminist thought, leading to a heightened awareness of diversity, evident in recent feminist literature, and an exploration into what is often called "intersectionality": the relationship between gender and other identities, especially race and class. Feminist theorists now understand that they cannot theorize gender without also taking race and class into account.[11] Critiques of universalism in feminist thought have also led to an increased awareness of social identity in general. A feminist can no longer write as if she is representing all women; instead she must acknowledge the identities that inform her perspective. This trend within women's studies has taken place within a broader context of multiculturalism throughout the disciplines.[12]

That is where this book comes in. My purpose is to ask how Jews fit into the feminist conversation about intersecting identities. Within women's studies, little attention has been paid to religion as a valid identity, and Jews have been noticeably absent from what is written about diversity. American Jews are not usually included in ethnic studies, but rather are seen as part of the white majority. As women of color have demonstrated, their experiences and perspectives as women are shaped by their racial identities. I contribute to this discussion by showing how Jews also have their own unique relationship to gender, influenced by their experiences and perspectives as Jews. And I add to the feminist dialogue about cultural difference and intersectionality by exploring the narratives of a group that has been absent from this discussion.

There is evidence in autobiographical writing that American Jewish feminists have recently begun considering the relevance of their Jewishness to their identities, experiences, and perceptions.[13] Many Jewish feminists who had previously identified themselves not as Jews but only as white women have begun to write about their Jewish identity in recent years, asserting its importance and noting their absence from feminist discussions of cultural difference.[14] Whereas previously they were a largely invisible, yet disproportionate, part of the women's movement, they are now proclaiming their Jewish identities and coming out of hiding.[15] People who had been writing for years as *American* feminists are now starting to write about being Jewish as well.[16]

Feminist Jews struggle to understand their place as Jews. Jewish second-wave feminists express a sense of dislocation both as feminists and as Jews and ask how being Jewish makes them different from other women. On the one hand, the vast majority of American Jews are white and thus occupy a position of privilege within the United States.[17] On the other hand, as Jews, they are members of a group with a long history of oppression. Anti-Semitism and the Holocaust are recurring themes in autobiographical writing by Jewish second-wavers.[18] Moreover, some of these writers claim that experiencing marginalization as Jews in the women's movement has caused them to question their place within feminist identity politics and to think more seriously about their Jewish identities.[19] Many of the themes that are raised in writings by Jewish feminists are also central to the interview narratives explored in this book.

Just as Jews have largely been absent from books about multicultural women, gender has been an undertheorized topic in sociological research on Jewish identity. The social scientific study of American Jews has only recently begun to sufficiently address questions of gender.[20] A small number of social scientists have studied particular groups of Jewish women.[21] This book contributes to the growing body of literature on Jewish women by offering a thorough and telling examination of the relationship between Jewish and feminist identities.

THE INTERVIEWS

I learned in school that convincing people to participate in research is very difficult, and yet, recruitment proved easy for this study. Apparently I touched on an issue that second-wave feminists had been waiting to talk about. They were fascinated with what being Jewish meant to them in the context of their activism, yet most had not delved into this topic before.

I tracked down my interviewees through a combination of methods: the snowball technique (each person I spoke to gave me the names of other potential interviewees), contacting those who identified themselves as part of my target population in writing, and posting a query on various e-mail lists. I submitted posts to a Judaic studies list, a Jewish feminist discussion list, and a women's studies list.[22]

After initial contact, I screened the correspondents to ensure that they had actually participated in the feminist movement during the 1960s and/or 1970s. People who identified as second-wave feminists but had not personally been part of any feminist action were not included in the sample.[23] People who had been feminist activists but did not label themselves feminists were also excluded. Before meeting with them, I tried to elicit details about both their Jewish and feminist backgrounds in an attempt to gather a well-rounded group of interviewees. So, for instance, toward the end of my data-collection phase, I only interviewed people who claimed to be practicing Jews in our initial correspondence, because I felt that I had already interviewed too many secular Jews and I needed to hear the perspectives of more observant Jewish feminists to round out the sample.

All thirty of the people I interviewed were Ashkenazi Jews of European descent. At the time of the interviews, they ranged in age from forty-seven to seventy-five, with an average age of fifty-nine. All were middle-class at the time of the interviews, but they had grown up with a mix of class backgrounds. They are a remarkably well-educated group; all but three have graduate degrees, and seventeen hold doctorates.[24] The interviews were confidential. Pseudonyms are used throughout the book to protect identities. Biographical sketches with more information on their life stories appear in the appendix.

I did not ask about sexual orientation during the course of the interviews, but some people volunteered this information. Six identified themselves as lesbians and two as bisexual. A number of others told me that they had identified as lesbians earlier in their lives but were married to men at the time of the interviews. Eighteen informants lived with heterosexual partners when the interviews occurred, and all but eight have children.

Since the purpose of my research was to explore the relationship between Jewish and feminist identities, I engaged in informal life history interviews so that I could observe the discursive construction of personal identities.[25] I asked the interviewees to describe their own life stories because identities are constructed as a process throughout the life course, and they change over time.[26]

I am interested in the meanings given to cultural discourses, and thus I asked broad, open-ended questions, allowing the tellers to define the response categories.[27] I used an interview guide only as a general framework rather than as a verbatim script. I did not ask all of the interviewees the exact same questions. The interviews were divided into three main sections: feminist autobiography, Jewish autobiography, and the relationship between feminism and Jewishness. Each interview lasted approximately two hours. Twenty-seven interviews were conducted in person, mostly at the informants' homes. Three interviews were conducted over the phone because it was not possible to meet in person.

The interviews started with the feminist autobiography because I felt that people would have an easier time discussing this aspect of their lives. This part of the interview was a recounting of the teller's feminist activist history. As a result, I learned much about the women's liberation movement—more details than can be reproduced in this book. I asked for this information for two reasons: to warm the teller up in the beginning of the interview and to ascertain the nature of feminist involvement in order to ensure a well-rounded sample in this regard. The Jewish autobiography section was also straightforward; it contained details about the interviewee's Jewish family background, practice, Jewish education, and feelings about being Jewish.

In the last section of the interview, I asked about the relationship between Jewishness and feminism, Jewish and feminist identities, and Jewish and feminist life histories. This section elicited narratives at varying levels of abstraction. Some people illustrated the relationship between their Jewish and feminist identities with vignettes, and others with more abstract ideas, through a theoretical discussion of the nature of Jewishness and feminism. Also, many interviewees linked their Jewish and feminist autobiographies earlier in the interviews, and thus it was not as difficult for them to tease out their understandings of the relationship between feminism and Jewishness at the end of the interview. All material in the interview accounts pertaining to both feminism and Jewishness became the focus of my analysis.

THE INTERPERSONAL COMPONENT

The apparent differences or similarities between researcher and study participants are always a factor in determining the outcome of research.[28] Like the participants in my study, I am both Jewish and feminist, and my informants seemed to take both for granted. There were clues that they saw me as an insider, part of their cultural group. For instance, they often used Hebrew or Yiddish phrases or referred to Jewish practices or facts that would probably be outside the frame of reference of a non-Jewish interviewer. The interviewees did not know that I attended Jewish schools for most of elementary and high school, yet they expected me to have the background to understand Hebrew, Yiddish, and religious references. They assumed that we spoke a shared language.

Although being a Jewish feminist means that I have much in common with my informants, my age sets me apart. I was twenty-seven and twenty-eight years old when I conducted this research, young enough to be the daughter or even granddaughter of the people I interviewed. The age difference did not usually feel like a factor in our interactions, but a few of the women apologized for acting like a "Jewish mother" with me: "I'm sorry to be such a Jewish mother, but be careful in the snow," they might say, or "Eat more," or "Wear your seatbelt." The stereotypical Jewish mother is extremely doting toward her children, to the point of being overbearing in her concern for their well-being.

When I resumed my interviews after a bout with the flu, I visited the home of a woman who epitomized this sort of interaction. Upon hearing my hoarse voice, she exclaimed that I sounded awful. She admonished me to drink more water, saying grimly, "Do you know how low the humidity is here? It's less than 10 percent. You have to drink at least a gallon a day." She sounded like she was scolding me for not taking care of myself. We went in the house, and she offered me all kinds of food from her kitchen. She then changed her mind about one particular offering, saying, "Oh, no, you can't have that. It's dairy." When I replied that I do, in fact, eat dairy, she insisted, "You can't! It will make you produce more mucus!"

This sort of interaction is more characteristic of participant observation than of the typical interview study, in which the researcher may meet with strangers for only a couple of hours for the interview session. Instead, I often had more extensive interactions with my interviewees. Although it was not officially part of my research design, any extended socializing beyond the bounded interview became a form of participation observation. I ate at restaurants with some of my informants before or after interviews, and many of the people I contacted who lived outside of New York invited me to stay at their homes when I visited their area. In these circumstances, I had the opportunity to observe people's lives, and they had the opportunity to become more comfortable with me.

Two of the women I stayed with took the time to "test me out" before being interviewed. One woman scheduled our interview for the end of my visit, after she had taken me out to dinner the preceding night and spent hours talking to me with her husband at her house. Before I left town, she explained that she had planned my visit this way because she had to make sure she trusted me before the interview, since she knew she would be talking to me about painful parts of her life experience.

Another interviewee, who also hosted me for a night in her home, had suffered from mental illness, and tried to gauge my attitudes toward mental illness prior to the interview. She took me out to dinner with her husband before the interview and asked me what I thought about a recent film,

Girl, Interrupted, which was about adolescent girls in a mental institution. All such experiences outside of the interview sessions became part of the fabric of my investigation and undoubtedly influenced my understandings of the people I studied.

INTERPRETING DATA

I began this research with the assumption that a Jewish feminist must feel at least some conflict between his or her Jewish and feminist identities. The tension between Jewishness and feminism was simply a given for me, and thus I took it for granted that others would feel the same. This is probably based on my own past experiences with such conflict. Also, everything I had heard and read pertaining to both Jews and feminism was based on a tacit assumption of incongruity. After all, the literature on Jewish feminism deals largely with religious issues and the conflicts that arise when feminists confront Judaism.

I recognized an important omission when I was interviewing Sam, one of the men in my sample. I realized that it had not previously occurred to me to actually ask people if they feel any tension between their Jewish and feminist identities. Perhaps I unconsciously considered it so obvious that I did not feel the need to ask about it directly. As soon as I became aware of this oversight, I asked Sam if he had ever experienced a conflict between his Jewishness and his feminism. I was surprised to hear him reply that he had not, followed by an elaborate explanation.

After that interview, I explicitly asked everyone who did not raise the issue themselves whether they felt cognitive dissonance, and I received a wide range of replies. My own personal biases had initially caused me to overlook an important area of inquiry. Luckily, I realized this blunder at an early stage of the interview process. This proved to be a significant aspect of my investigation.

It is important to keep in mind that putting the interview narratives in writing creates a false sense of fixity, belying the changeability and ambivalence inherent to social identities. Although the interviews are autobiographical, their retrospective nature is not intended to create a historical account. Instead, I am interested in the telling of life histories as windows into the informants' identities. Memories are by nature transient; we tell our histories from different vantage points at different times in our lives.

The scope of this study does not allow me to generalize about all Jewish second-wave feminists. In fact, it would be impossible to collect a representative sample of this group, because there is no comprehensive list of all Jews who participated in the women's liberation movement. In order to gather a representative sample, the researcher must know who is in the population from which the sample is to be drawn. It is not my intent to make general claims about this population, but rather to examine multiple discourses of Jewishness as they intersect with discourses of feminism. My larger aim is to think critically about the construction of cultural discourses and the integration of diverse identities.

ACTIVIST STORIES

The participants were involved in virtually all segments of the feminist movement of the 1960s and 1970s. The men belonged to feminist men's groups, protested violence against women, and supported reproductive rights and the Equal Rights Amendment. The women's feminist histories were more diverse. It was common for the women I interviewed to have had a range of affiliations in the women's liberation movement, either concurrently or over time.

Many participated in the radical feminist movement, joining informal collectives and communes. Some had been lesbian feminist separatists for a short period of time. Others participated in the less radical, liberal camps of feminism, and were active in their local chapters of the National Organization for Women. Still others were producers and performers within feminist theater and the women's music movement. Many of the interviewees were not active in any particular group but took part in an eclectic mix of feminist activities, such as consciousness-raising groups, newspaper collectives, battered women's shelters, marches, and demonstrations. Also, academic feminism, including women's studies, gender studies, and men's studies, had become a common career path for the people I interviewed.

Virtually all of my informants had also participated in other protest movements besides feminism, especially the civil rights and anti–Vietnam War movements. Feminism is seen as part of a larger worldview of political awareness and concern with social change. When I asked my interviewees to list the main elements of their identities, they used words such as "radical," "leftist," "progressive," or "activist," in addition to referring to themselves as feminists. My typical interviewee saw gender inequality as interconnected with racial, economic, sexual, and other systems of stratification. For many in the group, it was because they were already radicalized by the social movements of the 1960s that they joined the women's movement.

How did they become feminists? There is the typical story of the budding feminist who is finally able to make sense of her world through reading Betty Friedan's *The Feminine Mystique,* yet she hides it under her mattress so that her husband will not discover that she is reading such a scandalous book. And there are stories of being dragged by an already activist feminist friend to a speak-out or march. But most of the people I interviewed described a slower, less dramatic process that often began in their childhood—witnessing injustices around them or being inspired by their nontraditional mothers. Being raised in a liberal or radical household was certainly an influence on the adult proclivities of many of the interviewees.[29] However, it was just as common to hear about political consciousness born out of the counterculture of the student movements of the 1960s.

WHAT TYPES OF JEWS?

At the beginning of the interviews, I asked people to name the main elements of their identity. Some people gave a long list and some a short one. All of them mentioned being Jewish in their list of identities, even though I would come to discover a wide range of meanings attached to this identity. It is hard to know whether they would have listed "Jewish" if they were being interviewed on another, unrelated subject, or whether the Jewish self-labeling was a response to this particular interview topic. Yet, according to American cultural designations and the traditional Jewish definition of having a Jewish mother, all of the interviewees are Jewish. In every case, both parents were Jewish, and all but four (whose families have been in the U.S. for many generations) are the children or grandchildren of immigrants.

At the risk of simplifying a complex and changing identity, I can briefly summarize the Jewish identities of my research participants. None of the sample members are Orthodox, but all engage in at least some Jewish observances throughout the year. In fact, I was not able to find any Orthodox Jews identifying as feminists who had been activists in the women's movement in the 1970s. Why? Perhaps because Orthodoxy represents conservatism, and feminism represents liberalism. Only a highly unusual Orthodox woman would have had the gumption to become a feminist activist at that time. Today, on the other hand, there are many Orthodox Jewish-feminists who focus their activism on the Orthodox community.[30]

I felt it was important to interview people with a variety of Jewish backgrounds and religiosity, yet it was much easier to find secular than religious Jewish feminists. It was common for people who had been affiliated with the Left in the 1960s and 1970s to discard their religious affiliations. "Religion is the opiate of the masses," said Karl Marx, and many activists saw religion as regressive. Incidentally, a few interviewees even expressed concern that they would "skew" my findings because, in their minds, they were not Jewish enough, or not religious enough. They saw themselves as Jewish by culture, not by religion. They did not realize how typical they were among their Jewish second-wave feminist peers.

THE COMPLEXITIES OF AMERICAN JEWISH IDENTITY

There is ongoing debate about the definition of a Jew. Are Jews an ethnic group, a religion, both, or some other category? Richard Alba, in his landmark study *Ethnic Identity*, remarks upon the peculiar nature of Jewishness: "In contrast with other major religious groups in the United States Jews can view themselves as a 'people' and thus satisfy ethnicity's sine qua non."[31] Although for many Jews it would be difficult to tease out the ethnic from the religious components of Jewishness, others identify as Jews without practicing or believing in the religion of Judaism.[32] Jewishness includes, but is not limited to, the Jewish religion, encompassing ethnic identity and a history of cultural traits and practices as well as religious beliefs and customs.[33]

Yet "ethnicity" may not be the correct term to describe Jews, either. Sara R. Horowitz writes: "Current thinking in cultural studies considers Jews as a kind of ethnicity and defines this ethnicity as 'people from another place.' Unlike other ethnic groups (like Italian Americans, Irish Americans), however, Jews are not defined by where they come from but in spite of (or against) where they come from—and because of what they carry with them or what others assign to them (the idea that they are Jewish)."[34] Jewishness is a contested category and a special case. It is not quite ethnicity, not quite religion, and certainly not a monolithic category.

Any attempt to define Jewishness is further complicated by race. This book focuses on American Jews, the vast majority (but by no means all) of whom are classified as white because they are descended from Europeans. In this sense, most Jews currently enjoy white skin privilege in the United States; in Europe, however, Jews were, and in some places still are, defined as racial others. In present-day American Jewish culture, Ashkenazi culture is dominant. Many of the customs and traits that are thought of as "Jewish" are actually particular to the Ashkenazi tradition. Since everyone I interviewed is Ashkenazi and white, this research is not intended to be representative of American Jewish identity in all of its complexity. Furthermore, the cultural discourse represented in these interviews is specific to the United States; Jews in Israel, for example, would no doubt have a very different understanding of Jewishness with respect to gender and feminism.

As is true of any subculture, American Jews' ideas about themselves derive from internal and external sources, from both the telling of their own history and the perceptions of the larger culture. American Jewish identity is constructed through the individual's negotiation of Jewish cultural discourses as well as the discourses of multicultural America. Most American Jews are descendants of people who immigrated to the United States between 1880 and 1920, mainly from Eastern European countries. These immigrants fled persecution and poverty in Europe in search of freedom and economic opportunity in America. By the second and third generations, Jews living in this country had both ascended into the middle class and shed many of their immigrant ancestors' customs.[35] In America, Jews have achieved high levels of educational and professional attainment and have lived with relatively limited impact from anti-Semitism.[36] In fact, American Jewish women have attained higher levels of education than other American women and are more likely to participate in the labor force.[37]

Unlike Jews historically and currently living in other parts of the world, American Jews can affiliate with a variety of denominations, including Reform, Reconstructionist, Conservative, Traditional, various facets of Orthodoxy, and the lesser-known Jewish Renewal and Humanistic Judaism. The fragmentation of the American Jewish community, whether defined by denomination or otherwise, provides people with creative choices in terms of how to be Jewish. Any study of Jewish identity must take into account the variety of American Jewish cultural discourses produced by the plurality of Jewish communities.

FEMINIST ACTIVISM IN THE 1960S AND 1970S

The second wave of feminism is considered to have begun in the early 1960s and continued through the 1980s. As with any other social movement, scholars attribute its beginning to certain key events.[38] In 1961, President John F. Kennedy established the Presidential Commission on the Status of Women, chaired by Eleanor Roosevelt. The publication in 1963 of *The Feminine Mystique* by Betty Friedan (now perhaps the most famous Jewish feminist) is viewed as another major moment in the development of the second wave of feminism.[39] Both of these events were crucial to the beginning of the liberal feminist branch of the movement, which focused on reform within existing institutional structures. The central organization of the liberal branch of feminism is NOW, the National Organization for Women, founded in 1966 with Friedan as its first president.

In the late 1960s, the more radical branches of feminism appeared, with a more revolutionary goal. Whereas liberal feminism carried on the tradition of nineteenth-century feminists by calling for gender equality within the law, radical feminism aimed to do away with patriarchy completely. Radical feminists followed the practices of the student movements of the 1960s, including civil disobedience and decentralized grassroots collectives. In fact, many women were motivated to form women's groups after experiencing sexism in the civil rights and antiwar movements. An important organizing strategy of radical feminism was the creation of consciousness-raising groups, in which women met informally to discuss their everyday lives and understand the ways in which gender inequality had affected them. Most of the women I interviewed had participated, at least to some extent, in activities of the radical feminist movement.

The designation of the 1960s and 1970s as the second wave of the women's movement implies that the suffrage movement of the nineteenth century was the first wave of feminism, focused on gaining voting rights for women. Critics of the phrase "the second wave" point out that the women's movement did not start up again in the 1960s, but rather had been under way for decades, even if with less publicity. This was not a new movement, they argue, as much as a revitalized continuation of an ongoing women's movement. Although earlier feminism, spanning from the nineteenth century through the liberal women's movement of the 1960s, was focused on legal gains for women, radical feminism had a broader scope. This gave way to other branches of feminism, including Marxist feminism, which argued that gender inequality is inextricably linked with economic inequality, and the later emergence of black feminism, lesbian feminism, and other strands of thought that focused on linking gender to other axes of inequality.

There are many ways to categorize the branches of feminism, none of which do justice to the overlap between schools of thought and communities of feminists. Many of the people I interviewed simultaneously participated in the activities of multiple branches of feminism. Labels such as "radical feminist" and "Marxist feminist" do not designate distinct camps as much as convenient ways of understanding the history of the movement ideologies. These categories are not mutually exclusive, and feminists can move between different groups. For instance, there were very few purely "liberal" feminists in the group who did not later participate in radical, Marxist, or lesbian feminism.

Altogether, the gains of the various branches of the feminist movement have been massive—from constitutional amendments to new notions of what women and men can do and be. These gains were made by groups working together across ideological, gender, sexual, class, and racial differences.

JEWISH WOMEN'S RADICAL HISTORY

Jewish participation in the feminist movement of the 1960s and 1970s follows a long history of Jewish involvement in radical movements. These movements afforded Jewish women standing in the public sphere from which they had long been prohibited. Jewish women were prominent participants in revolutionary politics in Europe from the 1870s on.[40] Women were leaders and founders of the Bund, the Jewish socialist party, in the Pale of Settlement.[41] Later, Jewish women immigrants to the United States would become leaders in the labor union movement of the early part of the twentieth century.[42] Jewish women were also active in the suffrage movements in the United States, England, and other European countries.[43]

Following this tradition of political organization, it is not surprising that Jewish women played an important role in the women's liberation movement in the 1960s and 1970s. During that same period, Jewish women were also organizing to bring change to their own Jewish communities. Although American Judaism had already been slowly allowing women greater roles and improved status, the second-wave feminist movement inspired faster and more drastic change.

During the early 1970s, Jewish women mobilized within Jewish institutions using methods similar to those employed by the women's liberation movement, including consciousness-raising, to collectively demand change. In 1972, a group of Conservative Jewish women issued a "call for change" at the annual convention of Conservative rabbis, which eventually led to the decision to ordain women as rabbis and cantors in the Conservative movement. The first woman rabbi was ordained by the Reform movement in 1972, and the first Reconstructionist woman rabbi was ordained in 1974. A decade later, in 1985, the first Conservative woman rabbi was ordained by the Jewish Theological Seminary. Just as the women's liberation movement used conferences and other large gatherings to mobilize women, the Jewish-feminist movement convened a National Conference on Jewish Women in 1973 and then again in 1974.[44]

By the time the second-wave feminist movement arrived, many sectors of the Jewish community were ready and waiting for change; they just needed a push. For instance, in 1955, rabbis of the Conservative movement ruled in favor of calling women up to the Torah.[45] In 1972, however, only 7 percent of Conservative synagogues allowed it. Only four years later, in 1976, the percentage of Conservative synagogues that allowed women to be called to the Torah had gone up to 50 percent.

Synagogue life has changed drastically in the past thirty years as a result of Jewish-feminist work. Most synagogues now allow women equal participation in religious services. The role of women in synagogues varies greatly between movements. Nonetheless, today all Reform synagogues and the vast majority of Conservative synagogues grant women total equality.[46] No Orthodox synagogues are egalitarian, but even the Orthodox movement has been affected by feminist agitation; at least two women have received Orthodox rabbinic ordination, with more in training, and Orthodox congregations have begun to hire women spiritual leaders as "Congregational Interns."[47]

These trends—women's occupation of Jewish leadership positions and ritual equality in the synagogue—are tangible improvements in the structure of Jewish institutions that have resulted from the Jewish-feminist movement. The movement has also provided the space for women's creative and spiritual innovation, including the development of new rituals and Jewish-feminist cultural productions in such fields as art, literature, theater, and music. The availability of Jewish education to women and the ordination of women have added the perspectives of women to Jewish religious culture. On the academic front, Jewish-feminist scholarship has proliferated greatly in recent years. Whether scouring the Talmud with a gendered lens, uncovering the lives of women in Jewish history, or exploring the Bible from a woman's perspective, feminist scholars have provided a crucial framework within Jewish studies.

There is a tradition within Judaism of *makhloket,* arguing within the text. In the rabbinic tradition, the basis for most forms of contemporary Judaism, there are varying interpretations for each law and multiple readings of each issue. This tradition values questioning, even of itself, and the minority opinion is maintained within Jewish legal texts.[48] Each generation is given the opportunity to bring social factors into consideration in deciding religious issues.[49] Therefore, paradoxically, while the tradition emphasizes continuity with the past, it also makes room for innovation and has repeatedly done so throughout history, sometimes quite radically.[50] Although the Jewish-feminist enterprise is seen as dissenting from Jewish tradition, I contend that it is actually in line with the tradition: feminist interpretations of Judaism and feminist innovation in Jewish religious practice are within the bounds of the ancient Jewish tradition of innovation, questioning, and debate.

JEWISH-FEMINISTS VS. JEWS IN THE FEMINIST MOVEMENT

There is a crucial difference between the Jewish-feminist movement to transform Judaism that I have just described and the subject of this book—Jews who were in the women's liberation movement.[51] In fact, while Jewish-feminists were focusing their activism on the Jewish community in the 1970s, most of the feminists I interviewed were estranged from that community and experiencing their lifetime low point in terms of Jewish identity consciousness.[52] This trend has been noted by, among others, Sylvia Barack Fishman in *A Breath of Life: Feminism in the American Jewish Community:* "In the beginning many of the most active contemporary American feminists of Jewish birth devoted little attention to themselves as Jews (except occasionally to deride traditional Judaism as one more egregious example of patriarchal power)."[53] There seems to have been very little overlap between the cohort of Jewish-feminists who, for example, called for the ordination of women rabbis or became scholars of Jewish women's studies, and the population of Jewish women in the larger feminist movement of the 1960s and 1970s. When I was recruiting research participants, I found that most Jewish-feminists of the same age group now visible as feminists working within the Jewish community came to feminism a little later, in the 1980s.

Many of my interviewees explicitly discussed the influence of Jewish-feminism on their Jewish identities. No matter how secular or unaffiliated, the people I interviewed are aware of the difference between Judaism today and when they were growing up because of Jewish-feminism. Even for those who are detached from organized Judaism, these changes affect their understandings of the relationship between Jewishness and feminism. An important finding from my interviews is that despite the conflicts between Judaism and feminism, feminism and Jewishness are also seen as compatible. I doubt that this sentiment would have been so widespread if I had done my research twenty years ago, before the upsurge of Jewish-feminism. The existence of new feminist approaches to Judaism has paved the way for the kind of creative interweaving of identities that this book illustrates.

A NOTE ON STRUCTURE

Throughout this book, I present narratives from interview accounts that show various ways of navigating the relationship between Jewishness and feminism. There are four general approaches by which my interviewees negotiate their Jewish and feminist identities. They are described in chapters one through four.

The first approach, detailed in chapter one, is the integration of Jewish and feminist identities in the practice of religion. Some of the interviewees have channeled their activist energy into the feminist reconstruction of Judaism. This Jewish-feminist activism may take the form of participating in a feminist rewriting of Jewish liturgy, becoming a leader in a synagogue, or studying Jewish texts from a feminist perspective. Jewish observance becomes a mechanism for reconciling the dissonance between Judaism and feminism.

A second approach, discussed in chapter two, is adopted by those who envision their Jewish and feminist identities as complementary. The women portrayed in chapter two enunciate a theory on the parallels between Jewishness and feminism that I call the "discourse of Jewish-feminist congruence." They maintain that Jewish culture can be seen as compatible with feminism because both value social justice and question the status quo. They also link Jewish otherness and anti-Semitism to women's otherness and sexism. Some even claim that their feminism is rooted in their Jewishness.

Chapter three is about Jews' struggle to find a comfortable home in the feminist movement. In this chapter, I share interviewees' tales of marginalization, anti-Zionism, and anti-Semitism in feminist settings. Ultimately, these experiences led them to a sense of ambivalence about their place as Jews in feminist communities.

Whereas the first three chapters explore the narratives of Jewish feminist women, chapter four explores the construction of male Jewish feminist identities. Jewish profeminist men describe their perspectives on Jewish masculinity and its relationship to feminism. They see their Jewish and feminist identities as connected because both place them in a position of being outside mainstream society. They both articulate and critique what I call the "discourse of Jewish alternative masculinity." The gist of this ideology is that Jewish norms of masculinity are in line with feminist critiques of masculinity, and thus it is another paradigm of Jewish-feminist congruence.

The appendix presents a brief biographical sketch of each person presented in this book so that readers can turn there when they would like more information about a particular interviewee.

I have captured the ways in which people understand or talk about their Jewish and feminist identities and the intersections between them. Thus, this book is about narratives of identity. My framework for understanding these identities is not as individual psychological processes, but as products of the integration of cultural strands. This approach teaches us how activists make meaning out of their commitments to various communities. Individuals are faced with the challenge of integrating multiple identities; this study provides a context for examining the negotiation of these integrating challenges.

Chapter One

TORAH WARRIORS

Feminists Confront Religion

Rachel was cooking for the Sabbath when I arrived at her house on a Friday morning. There was a Hebrew-English Bible out on the table, which she was using to prepare a sermon that she would deliver in synagogue the next week. Rachel's Jewish practice is traditional. The stories she told me were infused with spiritual language. She talked about God perhaps more than any other interviewee did. She also became choked up with emotion at various points during our interview.

Rachel's religious life has helped her heal from many of the troubles of her past. She went through a turbulent time in adolescence and her early twenties, during which she was frequently arrested and was in and out of psychiatric hospitals. The Jewish community plays a key role in her life, giving her a sense of belonging after she had felt like a social misfit for so long. In the 1970s she turned toward Judaism after having "felt ripped off enough and disappointed enough by the revolution." She eventually became more religious through her involvement in a queer Jewish congregation.[1] Now she is an active member of three synagogues and feels valued by her Jewish community. Her way of practicing Judaism has become an extension of her activism.

When Rachel studies the Hebrew Bible and traditional Jewish texts, she focuses on the history of plurality within Jewish thought. She sees it as her mission to practice inclusive Judaism and teach others about it:

Well, being feminist affects everything about the way I'm Jewish, because . . . I'm not going to become a true believer in what somebody tells me is, well, this is the way to be Jewish. Number one: I know enough history to know there is no one way to be Jewish. And number two: I know that my God-given task is to push this in a way of including and recognizing and supporting women and prayers of various kinds. Including lesbians' reality and experience and wisdom and spirituality.

I see that as my role, like in the column . . . that I write for the [queer synagogue's] newsletter is for all these frequently Reform, or secular, or not very Jewishly educated Jews. To give them exposure to some of the wisdom that can be extracted from some traditional and Orthodox Judaism, and reformulate it in ways that leave out whatever really offensive elements can make it sometimes hard to get to in the first place. I see myself very much as a translator.

Translating Judaism is feminist activism for Rachel. It requires that she study feminist approaches to Jewish texts. She stresses the flexibility of Judaism: "Every *mitzvah* [Jewish commandment] that I learn about, there's some way to apply . . . You have to figure out how, and part of my work is figuring out how lesbian feminist American Jews of our generation can do it."

Rachel is highly knowledgeable about Jewish-feminist scholarship. She claims that she owes her participation within institutional Judaism as a lesbian feminist to the hard work of such scholars. Their work helps her interpret Judaism so that it is consistent with her other identities; she is not bothered by the ambiguities of her beliefs. She is quite comfortable with contradiction: "I've always been very good at believing incompatible things—ten preferably before breakfast. Because what else are you going to do? Like, sociologically, we're all marginal, right? There's nobody who's grounded in a single culture anymore. Why should I be?" When recalling her days in the women's liberation movement, she referred to herself as a "part-time atheist" even though she also believed that "all women are incarnations of the Goddess."

JUDAISM CHANGES

Although Judaism is historically rooted in patriarchy, and its laws and traditions exclude women from full participation in Jewish life, during the course of this past century American Jewish communities have radically changed the way they practice Judaism so that women now have opportunities that did not exist during the past five thousand years.[2] Although traditionally women were relegated to the role of passive observers in the synagogue, most synagogues outside of the Orthodox community are now gender-egalitarian.[3] Women can now count in a *minyan* (prayer quorum), are permitted to lead services, and are even ordained as rabbis and cantors.

While women have long been prohibited from public Jewish life, they currently serve in every capacity as leaders of Jewish communities. Furthermore, while traditionally women were permitted only a cursory education in Jewish texts, now even in Orthodox communities they have more access than ever before to serious text study.[4] Studying Jewish texts, especially the Talmud, requires a high level of Jewish education. To understand it properly, one must do more than merely open a volume of the Talmud and read it. Text study was traditionally prohibited for women in a gender-segregated culture, partly because it required teachers with skills in and received knowledge about particular methodologies of analysis.

Another transformation in American Judaism has resulted from the impact of feminism on Jewish thought.[5] Jewish-feminist scholarship has flourished in many areas in the past twenty years, leading to such developments as feminist interpretations of Jewish texts, Jewish feminist theology, gender-inclusive liturgy, and the creation of feminist rituals.[6] In many ways, Judaism is not the same religion as it was in the 1930s–1950s, when the participants in my study were growing up.

The Jewish-feminist movement made it possible for women such as those discussed in this chapter to practice Judaism as feminists. Although as children they were restricted in their participation in Jewish life, they can now play a role in the ongoing construction of Judaism and be leaders in their Jewish communities. Feminist activism takes different forms when the target is the Jewish community and Jewish religion. Some of the women I interviewed make feminist activism out of synagogue leadership, gendered liturgical change, and feminist text study—activities quite different from marching at rallies.

KNOWLEDGE IS POWER: FEMINISTS TAKE ON THE TORAH

In the Jewish tradition, Jewish education is obligatory and crucial to religious practice; studying the Hebrew Bible and traditional Jewish texts is a central *mitzvah*. In her study of the religious lives of elderly Jewish women in Jerusalem, Susan Starr Sered remarks on the salience of Jewish education: "According to Jewish belief there are certain deeds for which one is rewarded both in this world and in the next. These deeds are enumerated in the *Mishna* ('Peah' 1,1) and recited daily during the weekday morning prayer service: honoring one's father and mother, the practice of loving kindness, the making of peace between a man [*sic*] and his neighbor, 'but the study of Torah surpasses them all.'"[7]

While Jewish fathers are commanded to teach their sons Torah, the rabbis debated about the requirement, or even permissibility, of teaching daughters Torah. For much of Jewish history, only "exceptional" women were permitted to engage in the rigorous Jewish scholarship that was required of their brothers. During the twentieth century, however, this exclusion of women from Jewish education ended, and now, even in the most Orthodox sects, women engage in Jewish textual study.[8]

As women were welcomed into the realm of Jewish ritual leadership, they needed to acquire new skills. Allowing women to participate in public ritual life requires them to attain higher levels of Jewish education. For instance, in traditional Jewish services, trained congregants can chant from the Bible in Hebrew, using a musical form called cantillation. Women must also be familiar with Jewish texts and liturgy in order to deliver sermons. (In some synagogues, the congregants themselves deliver the weekly sermon, not the rabbi.)

Knowledge is power. For any previously subordinated group, education has been fundamental to the process of liberation. As women have become more Jewishly educated, they have fought to achieve more leadership. After a generation of girls had bat-mitzvahs, Jewish women began to argue on behalf of women in the rabbinate.

Once women started to occupy leadership positions in the Jewish community as rabbis and teachers, they provided their own standpoint on Jewish text. Women Judaic scholars have produced a wealth of scholarship with new ways of reading ancient texts. At the academic level, women's studies has made inroads into university Jewish studies departments. At the more local Jewish communal level, adult education series at synagogues and Jewish community centers now offer classes with feminist perspectives on Torah study.

Studying texts from a feminist perspective has become part of the activism of many of the women described in this chapter. Edith is a tireless advocate for the prominence of feminist rituals and programs in her synagogue and other Jewish institutions. Activism has been a constant in her life. She sees her activism as coming out of her Jewish upbringing: "As I look back on it . . . the fact that I was Jewish, the fact that there was a strong social action component in the Reform movement in the forties and the fifties, is part of my consciousness now. It is part of what informs my activism now."

During the period in her life when Edith divorced her husband and "came out" as a lesbian, she found a feminist rabbi who allowed her to see that she "could bring together Judaism and feminism." Her participation in Judaism has grown since then. Like many of the other women in this chapter, she was able to increase her involvement in Judaism in feminist contexts. She has devoted considerable energy to Jewish text study and participation in a gay and lesbian synagogue, including serving on the board, leading services, giving sermons, and organizing Jewish-feminist events. She now attends synagogue weekly.

Edith takes a deconstructionist approach to Jewish text study. She stresses the importance of highlighting the politically (feminist and otherwise) problematic areas in Jewish texts and struggling with them communally:

> There's a woman rabbi . . . who has had one of the greatest effects on how I look at Judaism and how I look at text. She says you look at text and you see what it has done. Damage it has done to women or damage it has allowed to do to women. And it's gotta be opened up and made public. And then you have to look at repairing it. And then make sure it doesn't happen again.
>
> And that is very, very, very much my approach to text. And my approach to what goes on in Judaism. And you can't keep glossing over it . . . And I've been part of this whole debate about whether you take some of this stuff out of Torah, or whether you leave it in and then talk about it and make it visible. And I've done some drashes for [my synagogue], and I feel that part of my job is to make it visible and show what's there and talk about it.

This type of interrogation of text is similar to the challenges faced by feminist scholars of any traditional canon, whether art history, Shakespeare, or the works of Freud. While struggling with the tradition is central to Edith's idea of what being a Jew is about, sharing what she learns in this struggle with others comes out of the feminist value of consciousness raising.[9]

Rachel, whose views on religion are presented at the beginning of this chapter, has engaged in feminist Torah study for many years. She endeavors to teach others feminist and progressive interpretations of Torah. She does this not through a formal teaching career, but through volunteering to speak about the weekly Torah portion during Sabbath services and volunteering to write in synagogue newsletters.

Janet, a librarian in her mid-fifties who is involved in multiple synagogue communities, highlighted the importance of feminist Torah study.

She spoke with sadness about her efforts to find a balance between Jewish tradition and feminist innovation. Janet is very involved in both a Conservative synagogue and a Jewish Renewal *chavurah*.[10] She finds that the former sometimes feels too traditional and the latter too "out there." She struggles with deciding where she feels closer. Janet has gotten more involved in Judaism since the 1980s and in the past ten years has become even more religious. She attends synagogue weekly and often leads services. She also takes adult Jewish education classes, which are frequently devoted to feminist topics.

Janet was the first girl to have a bat-mitzvah in her Conservative synagogue. She was chosen to set that precedent because she was skilled in Hebrew. At the time, she felt that this was a great honor, and it later became an important milestone in her life.

Janet recalled a trip she took to Israel with a progressive secular Jewish organization that was an influence on her reconnecting to Judaism as a young adult. She also used emotional language to describe how, through this organization, she was introduced to the Jewish-feminist movement: "I was starting to see again other models of what women were doing. And it struck chords with me . . . It was creatively interpretive and doing stuff that had to do with Judaism, and that had meaning behind it, and that included prayer, and that included arguing in terms of text, and that was interpretive. I mean, I loved studying Torah . . . And I battled for using feminist language, and it was that kind of thing . . . I started really feeling it inside. And that's when for me it became, you know, I'm a Jewish-feminist. I felt comfortable with it. I'm not a feminist who's Jewish; I'm a Jewish-feminist. I feel deep in my gut Jewish, and I feel deep in my gut feminist because of what I believe." Through studying Jewish text as an adult, Janet was able to view her Jewish self through an already acquired feminist activist's lens.

Janet has kept up with Jewish-feminist scholarship and has used Jewish-feminist tools for writing poetry and creating art. She enjoys attending classes that are dedicated to studying Jewish text from a feminist perspective. She repeatedly spoke about grappling with Jewish text, which seems central to her religious practice.

RITUAL LEADERSHIP AS FEMINIST ACTIVISM

The American women's movement began with a focus on equal rights. The ultimate goal was to put women in positions of power, such as mayor, senator, and corporate CEO. So when I was growing up, I thought feminism was about women becoming doctors and governors. In fact, I find that many of my undergraduate students are still stuck in that way of thinking. Women can do anything they want to do, they tell me: "My parents always told me I can have any career I wish. We don't need feminism anymore. We've already arrived."

This is the liberal feminist approach of dividing the pie into equal parts without changing its flavor. Men and women should be given the same opportunities, liberal feminists argue, and they successfully fought for educational and legal reforms to make this possible. Liberal feminists work within existing institutions to overcome discrimination against women, rather than challenging the social structure as a whole. It took radical feminism to more fully deconstruct the notion of gender and dig beneath the surface of how society operates. Instead, liberal feminists work within the power structure, playing by the rules of the system, to obtain greater representation for women in a male-dominated world.[11]

In the Jewish community, early feminist accomplishments followed the liberal feminist model of advancing women's roles within the system. Gains for Jewish women began this way in the 1950s, when girls like my mother were beginning to celebrate becoming b'not-mitzvah (plural of bat-mitzvah) in American synagogues. This coming-of-age ritual had been the exclusive privilege of boys being called up to the Torah for the first time. A major honor and lifecycle event, it was always in the masculine realm. Girls were not even allowed to bless the Torah or chant from it in front of the congregation. Only men had previously performed ritual roles in the synagogue. Along with the bat-mitzvah ceremony came women's increased participation in public ritual roles and therefore synagogue leadership. Gains were made for Jewish liberal feminism, culminating with the ordination of women as rabbis and cantors in the 1970s. These advances were a long time in coming: historian Pamela Nadell argues that changes in women's roles in the synagogue during the late nineteenth and early twentieth centuries helped pave the way for the ordination of women.[12]

Most of my interviewees grew up in the 1940s and 1950s, and some belonged to synagogues where they were among the first girls to become b'not-mitzvah. Others lived in communities where they were not allowed any ritual leadership or even formal Jewish education because of their gender. Consequently, for the latter group, leading rituals and participating in synagogue leadership are often experienced as highly empowering adult experiences. Though their participation was made possible by the feminist movement, they see it as a form of feminist activism in and of itself. This notion of feminism, as rooted in equal access to public roles, is classic liberal feminism, and it provides a framework for understanding Jewish observance as contributing to the empowerment of women.

Natalie, a lawyer and a writer, expressed this liberal feminist notion of Jewish progress. She wanted to be a rabbi when she was younger, partly because it was a profession that was not available to women. She claims that she was "not able to make that leap of imagination," so she chose law, another male-dominated profession. Natalie is very active as a board member and volunteer for her participatory synagogue and in other Jewish activities.[13] She has become more observant over the years, partly as a result of participating in her synagogue. She says about her increasing involvement in Jewish life: "So that's like a whole part of my life that's been really, really fulfilling for me."

Natalie did not grow up in a Jewish community where girls and women could participate equally. As a small child, she attended an Orthodox synagogue daily with her great-grandfather and sat in the men's section. She describes the experience in superlative terms: "And it was just incredible. I just thought this was the most wonderful thing I'd ever seen—even as a very, very young child." Then, when she was twelve years old, she was moved to the women's section, as is the Orthodox custom for girls entering puberty. She described this experience as being "kicked out" of the men's section and "traumatic." She would never again attend an Orthodox synagogue. Although she encountered the sexism in traditional Judaism at a young age, the experience obviously did not permanently alienate her from the religion.

Natalie does not take for granted the achievements of the Jewish-feminist movement. She feels privileged to be an active member of a participatory congregation, because it enables her to play roles that were not possible for women in the past: "So for me, one of the really important things has been to spend time developing skills that were restricted in the past that I didn't have the opportunity to learn to do. And I'm doing things now like *haftarah* chanting.[14] I sort of feel like I'm doing things that in the past were not available to women, and it's really important for me, as a woman, to do that; as well as it's just very personally satisfying." Natalie frames women's participation in Judaism itself as a feminist act. Like many of the other women, she told me that she gets very emotional each time she is called up to the Torah in synagogue just knowing that women were not allowed to do so for thousands of years. Her awareness of her newly found rights is a motivating factor for her Jewish practice. In the broader society, liberal feminism paved the way for women to join men in the boardroom, while in the American synagogue the result was more women on the *bimah*.[15]

Rosalyn, who is married to a Reform rabbi, also began her feminist autobiography in an Orthodox synagogue. Her father was Orthodox, so the family belonged to the Orthodox synagogue and attended services there. Rosalyn was unhappy with her subordinate status: "We were separated out . . . I would go to junior congregation, and the only thing I could do was prayer for the country . . . I mean, that's what the girls did. And I was the top student in Sunday school . . . I was the valedictorian. I just didn't like the attitude towards women there." Later, as a teenager, she joined a youth group at a Reform synagogue. There she learned about the value of social justice in Judaism; they studied Albert Vorspan's *Justice and Judaism: The Work of Social Action* (1956), which "raised my social consciousness." Rosalyn mentioned this book at various points during the interview. She feels that her training in social justice at this synagogue was the root of her subsequent feminist activism.

Rosalyn remembers that the restrictions on girls' religious training at her Orthodox synagogue displeased her greatly: "I guess I could have had a bat-mitzvah or something . . . But I didn't want to have a bat-mitzvah and not be able to read from the Torah. I'd rather not do it than do it halfway. I mean, that bothered me a lot." Her memories of the gender inequality she experienced there have made her appreciative of the equality in her current temple: "I mean, when we have *Simchas Torah*, it's a thrill to carry the Torah around . . . To think that I can do that when I could never do it before. I don't think that everything listed in the Torah is so hotsy-totsy. I even have questions about things like that . . . Still, it's the Torah, and to carry it around is such an honor. And when we were left out of that, I hated that. And now all the women here, they all want to carry it if they can. So that's good."[16] During the 1970s, Rosalyn was a leader in her local and state-level NOW chapters. Thus, it is not surprising that she would describe the gains of the Jewish-feminist movement in clearly liberal feminist terms: "In terms of equality of opportunity and synagogue life, well, look—we've seen how that's changed. How many presidents of temples are women . . . My God; you think about from 1970 to now, the past thirty years, all the women cantors and rabbis and all that stuff!"

The liberal feminist view of gender and Judaism focuses on the gains made for women in terms of "equality of opportunity" such as ritual leadership and ordination, without an examination of the underlying system of gender in Judaism. A radical feminist view would counter that just because women are now permitted to engage in new roles does not mean that the patriarchal institution of Judaism has been transformed. Also, gains for women have not been made across the spectrum of Jewish communities. While most Conservative and all Reconstructionist and Reform congregations allow women equal participation, Orthodox synagogues still do not.[17] Furthermore, recent studies have found gender discrimination within the structure of Jewish communal organizations such as community federations.[18]

DECONSTRUCTION AND RECONSTRUCTION

Some of the women I interviewed are not satisfied with increasing the numbers of women rabbis or seeing more women leading synagogue services. These feminists have a more radical critique of the gendered nature of Judaism. Just as the radical branch of the women's liberation movement was aimed at overcoming patriarchy as a whole, these Jewish feminists are unable to fully reconcile themselves with the patriarchal base of Judaism.[19] They question the portrayal of women in texts, the marginalization of women's experiences, and androcentrism in Jewish thought. Unlike those who take the liberal approach to Jewish-feminism discussed above, these women continue to question and struggle with Judaism through more extensive deconstructionist thinking.[20] Their approach supports Judith Lorber's definition of radical feminism's take on religion: "In *religion*, radical feminism argues that while more women clergy and gender-neutral liturgical language are very important in reforming religious practices, they do not make a religion less patriarchal unless there is also a place for women's prayers, rituals, and interpretations of sacred texts."[21]

Rebecca, an academic feminist, is old enough to have been denied a Jewish education because she was female, although her brothers celebrated bar-mitzvahs. She was not affiliated with Judaism for many years, including her days in the women's liberation movement. When her son was a young child, she decided to join a Reform synagogue so that he could attend Hebrew school and become a bar-mitzvah. She began to study Judaism on her own by reading the books he brought home from that school. She eventually became involved in the synagogue and began learning more about Judaism; she taught herself Hebrew and to read the prayers.

Rebecca explains that this transformation took place in coherence with her feminism: "I got interested almost as an intellectual pursuit. And then

Jewish-feminism started surfacing and then I got interested in that as well
... And so I started going to different services and really educated myself
in Judaism. And then, at the same time, in feminist issues that were coming up—liturgy changes. And so it was kind of everything was all together,
being a mother and being a feminist and being Jewish." Rebecca continued
her synagogue affiliation and leadership after her son grew up and moved
out of her home. She has changed synagogues a few times but has remained
active and has even served on a synagogue board.

Rebecca's adult reconnection with Judaism began at a time when the
Jewish-feminist movement was flourishing, which provided her with a way
"in" that was congruent with her identity: "I think that if I couldn't have
been feminist and Jewish, then I wouldn't have been Jewish." Rebecca
insists that she would not join a congregation that is neither Reform nor
Reconstructionist. Joining a synagogue with a feminist woman rabbi was
instrumental to her religious path: "Would I have become as active in Judaism? I suspect that I would have dropped out of Judaism . . . if I hadn't
discovered Rabbi ____ and joined the temple I'm in now." Rebecca has
been a consumer of Jewish-feminist literature. She is "interested in feminist
interpretations of Torah." She implemented gender-sensitive curricula as the
president of a synagogue school. She has also brought a feminist perspective to her other leadership positions within synagogues over the years.

I asked Rebecca whether she feels cognitive dissonance between being
Jewish and feminist. Her reply reveals a radical feminist unease with the
patriarchal current in Judaism: "One of the things that one of my friends
raises, she feels that you're never going to clean up the patriarchy in Judaism. She doesn't care how much you clean up the language. It's a patriarchal
religion, period. And there are times when I feel, what am I doing here?
. . . You know, I'm an atheist [uneasy laugh] in the sense that I don't go
to synagogue to pray. I like the liturgy. I like ritual and I like the liturgy
and I like the knowledge and I like being part of the community. But there
is a, when you say cognitive dissonance, there is this kind of, you know,
bracketing off of—yes, it is a patriarchal religion . . . there *is* a cognitive
dissonance." Even with the advances that have been made by the Jewish-
feminist movement, Rebecca is claiming, the underlying system of Judaism
is still flawed. She sees the religion itself as hopelessly patriarchal.

Nonetheless, Rebecca justifies her observance of a patriarchal religion by
placing it within a social and historical perspective: "The major religions
are gendered. And because they are gendered, they legitimize the gender
division and the gender hierarchy. So that religions, all the major religions,

are very much part of a legitimation of the patriarchal underpinnings of our society . . . I could never become a Wiccan [laughing] or anything like that; I would like to become part of a Jewish-feminist congregation . . . That's what I would really like." With the statement that all of the major religions are patriarchal, Rebecca places the problems of Judaism in perspective. In addition to her claim that Judaism is no more patriarchal than those other religions, she points out that it is changing because of the feminist movement. However, Rebecca asserts that the radical feminist approach is limited in its powers of reconstruction. It can go only so far.

Sarah, on the other hand, claims that her Jewish observance has been informed by feminism since before her bat-mitzvah. She says that growing up in the Conservative movement made her feel that "Judaism was an evolving and changing thing." She was an activist in the early abortion rights movement. She is a religiously observant Jew who adheres to the Sabbath and dietary laws. As a teenager, Sarah remembers feeling that "there were no inconsistencies between [being] a good feminist and being a good Jew. It was just a question of working for greater enfranchisement of women within the Jewish community." In other words, she was content to place Judaism within a liberal feminist framework as a young woman, even though that is no longer the case.

Over time, Sarah has moved to a more radical perspective on gender and Judaism. She has come to feel that Judaism is essentially irreparable because of the patriarchal roots of the rabbinic legal structure. It seems that the more she has learned about Judaism, the more critical she has become and the more dissonance she has experienced. Although Sarah works hard to integrate feminism into her Jewish practice, she is still deeply dissatisfied. She described feeling increasingly so for the past few years.

It was difficult to pin down the extent of Sarah's critique, because she vacillated between describing Judaism as a hopelessly flawed system and expressing that perhaps a feminist reconstruction of it is possible. She is torn between her commitments to both the old and the new, between traditional Jewish customs and feminist ideologies. "And I also sometimes think . . . that honestly trying to turn Judaism into a feminist enterprise is an attempt to do something completely inauthentic to it that won't make it recognizable in terms of continuity as Judaism . . . And then I have this very painful choice of deciding if I'm ready to part with it. And I'm probably not. But I think that Judaism can change. But I really think that there's some stuff that's so patriarchal down to its core that we've all been afraid to look at lest we be put up against this issue of, Can we really stay here?

Is there anything left to work with? We're talking about an authority structure that's alien to feminism as I see it." Sarah's perspective is similar to Rebecca's in that their questioning of Judaism is extensive. They offer the radical feminist deconstruction of a religious system without the certainty of reconstruction.

Sarah is ambivalent about the possibility of "fixing" Judaism. She is pessimistic about the transformative possibilities of feminist creativity within Judaism such as liturgical reform, and calls it "tinkering," even though she has taken part in it herself. She argues that Jewish-feminists have made only superficial adjustments and that they "haven't done enough with the paradigms that are operating underneath." In other words, she is critical of the liberal feminist approach to Judaism. Heterosexism within Judaism is central to her critique: "Until the Jewish community is willing to look at alternatives to heterosexual dyads, and I mean both things—heterosexual and dyads—Jewish-feminism hasn't got a lot to offer me. I feel like all that's really happened is the doors that used to be closed to women are now open to them. But it's still a patriarchally conceived world of artificial dichotomies. And that Jewish feminists haven't really, for the most part, haven't fundamentally challenged that . . . I mean, I think some interesting stuff has the potential to happen now. But for the most part, it's been about getting women into the rabbinate, getting women into the cantorate, and liturgical reform. *And that just don't cut it, baby* [said in an exaggerated, emphatic whispered tone, followed by laughter]."[22]

Despite Sarah's radical feminist approach, she is still ambivalent about how to move forward and resolve the problems of Judaism. She claims that she is in the vanguard in terms of the depth of her probing of Judaism while maintaining a deep attachment to Jewish tradition: "I think it's partly that I really do want to keep the old. I think, a lot of the old. I think a lot of people who are into new rituals, new liturgy . . . do not love the Hebrew language and the traditional prayers, all of those things, as much as I do. Don't have that imagery sort of engraved on their hearts the way I do. I wouldn't be comfortable bailing out for something completely new. It wouldn't feel like it had a Jewish character, to me, anyway . . . I am worried that the place that I belong constantly invalidates me as a human being. Wipes me out as a human being. I belong there and I have that comfort of home, but it's like getting comfortable with your oppressor."

Sarah is currently in a phase of deep questioning after a lifetime of feminism and Jewish practice. Her attempt to reconcile her Jewish and feminist selves is clearly painful for her. She is in the difficult position of being stuck between her radical critique and her love of traditional Judaism. She does not want to be too innovative in her Jewish observance because she is wedded to traditional customs. She is still searching for something "authentically Jewish and thoroughgoingly feminist" since she does not feel that most existent Jewish feminist scholarship lives up to that goal. Sarah fantasizes about going back to school to immerse herself in Jewish studies in order to work on this problem.

Like Rebecca, Naomi grew up before any females were given access to Jewish education and ritual leadership. Consequently, she did not learn Hebrew until she was an adult. Naomi is a writer who has written about and for Jewish women. She thinks of herself as a pioneer of the Jewish-feminist movement.

Naomi used the words "battle" and "fight" repeatedly to describe her struggles with Judaism and the Jewish community. Nonetheless, she says, "I never disassociated myself from being Jewish." Even during the 1960s and 1970s, when so many of her cohort became unaffiliated Jews, Naomi tried to find a place for herself: "I'm a *shul* [Yiddish for synagogue] goer . . . I would go from *shul* to *shul*. I never heard a rabbi who didn't demean women. I walked out . . . So I would try so hard to be a nice Jewish girl and they wouldn't let me."

When I asked her about the tensions she feels as a Jew and a feminist, Naomi talked about the hostility toward feminism that she has encountered among Jewish male leaders. For instance, during a class, she fought with a rabbi who wanted to teach *Ethics of the Fathers,* a text she called "insulting" to women. She spoke with anger about being in a "constant battle with terrible text."

Naomi stresses the necessity of the ongoing questioning and challenging of one's own religion and community. As Jewish feminist theologian Judith Plaskow writes, "The decisions to struggle with Torah, to criticize it, to remain in relation to it, all presuppose a more complex attitude."[23] This type of deconstruction is feminist activism to Naomi: "So even if you're Jewish, you can't sit back. You challenge and you stretch and you become insider and outsider. You don't just walk around being Jewish. You have to walk around outside of Jewish, and you have to say, 'What is that? What's happening over there? Who are those people? Are some of those people my enemies? Actually they are.'"

After the many conflicts that Naomi has experienced with male Jewish leaders, the anger she feels is clear:

It's still our fight. We don't have anybody to help us . . . And it's very painful to have to fight that battle. Twenty years I've been fighting that battle. When people say something and make a remark, I think: Do I have to educate you? My breasts dried up long ago; I don't want to nurse you anymore.

So I find much more sympathy for feminism among non-Jews, among men who are not Jewish than among Jewish men. They are not our allies in this movement . . . When I . . . helped bring the Torah to the [Western Wall in Jerusalem] and I saw who rose and cursed us and what they said to us, I thought, son of a gun, my own are my enemies. That's an interesting fact to find out.

The incident at the Western Wall refers to ultra-Orthodox men cursing at women who were transgressing the norms of their community by holding a women's prayer service at this holy site.[24] Naomi suggests a woman-centered approach to feminist activism in Judaism. She clearly feels that she and other Jewish women have to struggle to create change on their own, without the support of Jewish men. Similarly, radical feminists argued that placing women in the center is necessary for rethinking traditional disciplines and canons in the academy and that feminism should be fought *by women* on behalf of women.

Although Naomi's narrative is colored with bitterness, she is nonetheless optimistic about the future of Jewish-feminism. She is proud of the burgeoning field of Jewish-feminist scholarship, and stated that she had "helped birth all of that." Naomi's story is about her personal efforts and successes in effecting change. She sees transformative possibilities in the efforts of Jewish-feminism. When I asked her why she has remained involved in Judaism, she answered: "You choose your fights, right? I fought [for] civil rights, I fought the war. I fought for feminism, I think. To make Judaism something else. And it will be, it will be something else, it's changing. It's gonna be something else. It's just there have to be more women rabbis. And they are changing things. So that's very nice. Wouldn't it be nice if that were the last thing I fight?"

The stories of these women show that it is possible to transform religious practice into feminist activism. Once the activist energy of the 1970s was over, Judaism provided a locus for feminist activism, mobilizing the interviewees beyond their previous activist milieu. I am using the concept of activism here in its broadest sense, to mean a collective push for social change. The methods of mobilization and the routes to change may not be conventional. Typically, activism includes such activities as letter-writing campaigns, public demonstrations, and sit-ins. Although Jewish-feminists have used these methods to make changes in Jewish communities, they are more likely to express their activism by leading synagogue services, becoming rabbis, and studying Jewish text from a feminist perspective.

The women described thus far in this chapter actively work, through their religious observance and Jewish communal leadership, to bring together Jewishness and feminism. They are Jewish-feminists; their Jewish religious practice is a site of their feminist activism. They are part of the development within Judaism of feminist-inspired and gender-egalitarian religious observance. Not only are they keenly aware that they occupy positions and roles within their Jewish communities that were previously barred for women, but they also see this newly permitted participation as a feminist act.

A number of common themes arise in their stories. All of the women discussed here use Torah study as a tool for engaging with Judaism as modern women and as feminists. Synagogue leadership provides a venue for engagement with the Jewish community, allowing them to make feminist inroads into Jewish institutions. The process of the feminist transformation of Jewish liturgy has also played an important role in the religious practice of some of the interviewees. Their participation in synagogues and Jewish text study has been facilitated by important figures, most importantly the women rabbis who have served as valuable role models for their Jewish-feminist journeys.

Many religious Jews who went through the life-changing experience of the women's liberation movement concluded that Judaism is not for them and that feminists cannot be practicing Jews. But the women discussed above actually became more religious, more observant, or more deeply involved in Judaism after participating in the women's liberation movement. These women all have a deep love for the Jewish religion; being Jewish is more than a cultural identity for them. They are all practicing Jews, members of synagogues, and volunteers for leadership positions in their local Jewish communities. They also are all active learners and keep up with Jewish-feminist and other modern Jewish scholarship, which helps them practice Judaism as critical thinkers, progressives, and feminists.

Since these women are religious, to varying degrees, they do experience tension between their Jewish and feminist identities. This is inevitable because their identities draw on an ancient religious system that does not easily translate into a new ideology such as feminism. However, their narratives are not just about conflict; they are also about actively working to join Jewishness and feminism. They bridge the gap between Jewish practice and feminist orientations through their creativity and spirituality and with their participation in Jewish-feminist rituals, Jewish education, and synagogue leadership. Their adult Jewish observance is dependent upon the Jewish-feminist movement, and they relate to Jewishness from this perspective. I would venture to guess that many of them would not have been as religious as adults if Jewish-feminism had not come about.

REJECTING THAT WHICH REJECTS YOU

So far in this chapter, we have heard the stories of Jewish feminists who have continued to grapple and struggle within Jewish religious institutions. Others, however, have been so turned off by the sexism in Judaism that they have chosen to disengage completely.

There is a popular narrative among feminists about the "click moments" in life, those experiences that cause you to say, "Aha, now I get it! I suddenly see the sexism in the world." The proverbial light bulb comes on in your head when you are observing your everyday life. All of a sudden, you start to take notice of gender inequality. It has always been there, but you are just now recognizing it. From this moment on, there is no turning back. Your consciousness has been raised. There is no choice but to act on this newfound knowledge and protest the inequality that you see around you. Henceforth you will be a feminist.

Some Jewish women experienced such a click moment early in their lives in a Jewish setting. It may have been instigated by exclusion from leadership positions, unequal treatment from brothers or male peers, or negative experiences with rabbis. It may have happened when they were reading a translation of the Bible in synagogue or learning the meaning of the words in the prayer book. All of these types of experiences were recounted as part of the feminist journey for the women I interviewed. Unfortunately, experiencing sexism within the Jewish community often left a negative impression upon Jewish women in previous generations. Some of the women I interviewed would not join a synagogue or attend Jewish services after their childhood experiences. On the basis of their stories, it is hard to know whether they would have been affiliated Jews without such experiences. Memories are constructed through a teller's current frame. I find it significant, however, when an interviewee attributes a decision as momentous as leaving the religion of Judaism to experiencing sexism during childhood.

Just as Jewish feminists have often struggled with their place in feminist communities, they have struggled with their place in Jewish communities. These women were raised in an era when gender roles were extremely limiting for girls. At times, they experienced the discord between their own self-concepts and others' gendered expectations as coming from within Jewish culture. Some also experienced sexism and violence at the hands of Jewish men. These experiences were not about the dissonance between Jewish religion and feminism, but they nonetheless can be understood as pointing to clashes between Jewish experiences and feminist perspectives.

Jennifer, a retired academic feminist, spoke of such experiences. Jennifer's Jewish identity is complex, born out of both positive and negative experiences in her Jewish upbringing. She grew up in a heavily Jewish urban community and was actively involved in her synagogue, winning religious school awards and graduating as salutatorian of the synagogue's school. However, a number of negative experiences in her life, involving Jewish men, rabbis, and spiritual questions, pushed her away from the organized Jewish community. As an adult, Jennifer has made periodic forays into participating in Jewish organizations, but she has always left disappointed. Her disappointment is not only about gender; she also expressed bitterness about the current American Jewish community around issues of racism and able-ism. She does not belong to a synagogue or participate in formal Jewish activities or institutions.

Despite Jennifer's antipathy toward institutional Judaism, her Jewish identity seems integral to the way she presents herself. In fact, another informant, Randi, who knows Jennifer but was unaware that I had interviewed her, mentioned Jennifer to contrast her own submerged Jewish identity with Jennifer's "out-front" and "dominant" Jewish identity. In the beginning of the interview, when I asked Jennifer what names she applies to herself, she replied: "You know how Cynthia Ozick says, 'Everywhere in the world, I'm a Jew except in *shul* [synagogue], and there I'm a woman'? So, yeah, Jew and woman are the twin identities. And which one is dominant depends on the context." Jennifer views Jewishness as an essential cultural identity and maintains that her Jewish identity is foremost in her self-concept.

Jennifer's early feminist autobiography relates to her realization of the confinement of her role as a Jewish female. When I asked her where her feminist autobiography began, she told a story from her childhood. When she was five years old, she walked into a room and found her uncle comforting her father. She worriedly asked her father what was wrong, and her uncle replied, "I was just consoling your daddy because he'll never have somebody to say *Kaddish* for him."[25] When Jennifer asked him what he meant, he told her that her mother was not going to have any more children. Because she would be the only child, and, her uncle explained, "because only a boy can say *Kaddish*," her parents would die without anyone to say this memorial prayer in their honor.

Jennifer told the remainder of this early childhood story from her adult perspective: "And I said, 'Do you mean to tell me that your son . . . can do something I can't do?' And my uncle said, 'Yeah, he's a boy; he can say *Kaddish*. You can't say *Kaddish*.' And so I was made inarticulate with rage by that. I kicked him very hard in the shins!" As a grown woman, Jennifer remembers this experience with pride because it shows that even as a young child, she fought against sexism.

When I remarked to Jennifer that it is interesting that her feminist autobiography began with this Jewish moment, she said, "Oh, absolutely! And so here's another one." She then proceeded to tell me another story connected to her Jewish upbringing that contains a lesson about gender roles. Jennifer was friends with a neighborhood boy who was the son of a rabbi. The rabbi took an interest in her, and they would take walks around the neighborhood together. As an intellectually precocious child, Jennifer was flattered by the rabbi's attention and assumed that he was interested in her keen mind, so she took the opportunity to ask him creative and challenging questions about Judaism. She recounted a few of them to me, which included protests of the problematic portrayals of biblical women.

Jennifer's retrospective interpretation of the rabbi's interest in her leaves her feeling disappointed. She wanted to grow up to be a rabbi herself, but it seems that the neighborhood rabbi was interested in her as a candidate to marry his rabbi-to-be son—two very different plans. Jennifer recalls that when he could no longer find answers to her challenging questions, "he'd reach over and he'd stroke my hair and he'd say, 'Oy, [Jenneleh], you're such a *sheina maydel* [pretty girl]. You'll grow up and you'll be a good *rebbetzin* [rabbi's wife].'" Jennifer remembers this story in detail; it played a significant role in the development of both her Jewish and feminist identities. Her interactions with this rabbi taught her a lesson about the limited abilities she had within Judaism and stifled her Judaic intellectual aspirations.

Later in her life, as a young woman, Jennifer had another negative experience with a rabbi. When she became engaged to a gentile man, her mother urged her to go see a rabbi, insisting that she probably would not be happy in this marriage because she had always been so actively Jewish. So Jennifer agreed to speak to her childhood rabbi. Although she had been one of the top students in the synagogue, the rabbi did not remember her name. Jennifer angrily recounted the episode: "You'd think the guy would know me. He had handed me any number of prizes and awards in front of the congregation." Instead, the rabbi immediately asked her about her male friend from Hebrew school to whom she was always given second place: "And then I understood the whole history—why he was valedictorian when I was salutatorian, why he got first prize and I got second prize. I was pissed beyond belief! This is another of my Jewish feminist moments . . . I abandoned institutional Judaism after that last meeting with Rabbi ____, when he asked me how [the boy] was. And I've only very, very sporadically, for very short periods of time, been involved with institutional Judaism of any sort since then."

Rabbis are seen as official representatives of Judaism and thus can have a significant impact on congregants' feelings about being Jewish, with even the most casual interaction. Rabbis are apparently often unaware of the repercussions of their interactions with young women and the potential to make an impact, either positive or negative, on their ongoing Jewish identities. Once again, Jennifer was left feeling that her importance was diminished because of her gender; neither rabbi recognized this young girl's intellectual potential. Jennifer points to this experience as the final straw in her frustrations with Judaism. In her memory, she actually dropped institutional Judaism at that point in time.

Alice, a social worker, also feels antagonistic toward the Jewish religion because of the way women's roles have been presented to her. She feels that her Jewish identity has "developed more" as she has gotten older. Nonetheless, she maintains that she is "Jewish culturally and not religiously" and would almost consider herself antireligious. She said that she has a "love/hate relationship" with Judaism: "I've never been ashamed of being Jewish; I'm proud of being Jewish. I just can't deal with the religion."

Alice grew up with traditional gender roles. She feels that she was raised to be a "good Jewish girl," which meant getting married and having children. Once she accomplished that, it was clear that her role would be as passive wife and family peacekeeper. Those were her mother's plans for her: "That's what a Jewish girl/woman was supposed to be. You're supposed to let your husband take care of you. And no matter what, whatever it is, you make it all right. So that was the idea I grew up with as a Jewish female—Jewish womanhood." Consequently, Alice's mother was worried when Alice did not get married until her mid-twenties. Later, when Alice divorced her husband, her mother tried to talk her out of it because she worried that Alice would have no one to take care of her.

Alice sees the gender dynamics within her family as typical of a Jewish household, even though others might attribute them to the time period: "I have an older brother who was the crown prince in the house, and everything was lavished on him. And that was basically my Jewish sense. And my male/female sense. As a female, I was the lesser. [My brother] got everything; [he] got the praise, got opportunities, got the attention. And I got what was left." This interpretation of Jewish gender roles is certainly one among many. Other people I interviewed made a contrasting claim—that Jewish girls were raised with loftier goals and possibilities for greater aspirations than other girls.

Alice is highly offended by the treatment of, and attitudes toward, women in Orthodox Judaism, which seems to be her only exposure to religious practice: "Even though there wasn't Orthodoxy in my home, I was aware of it growing up in the community, and I was always very confused by this idea of why couldn't men and women sit together in the temple? And why did women have to be covered all the time? And all of these things which I find incredibly, incredibly offensive."

Alice's brother became Orthodox as an adult, and she has had a great deal of friction with him and his family over their different relationships to Judaism: "There was some family occasion where we had to go to temple. And they were very Orthodox. And my sister-in-law was sweating, she was so worried that [I] was going to cause a scene, 'cause I had to sit behind the curtain. And I was a good little girl. I did what I had to do, hating myself for it afterwards."

Alice's experiences with Orthodox Judaism and the traditional gender roles within her family have left her unable to see any congruence between the Jewish and feminist aspects of herself. When I asked her how Jewishness and feminism relate, she said:

> I knew there was a group of women called Jewish-feminists. And to me that was an oxymoron. I couldn't understand how the two could coexist. To be Jewish meant that, to me, that you could not be a feminist . . . My view of Jewishness was Orthodoxy. And Orthodox women could not be feminists, are not feminists. No matter how much they say they run the household and that's their realm.
>
> It's a division, it's not equal, it's not shared. It's not—I mean, the idea of, why are they covered up? Why do they have to wear wigs or head coverings? The reason is so that they're not seductive to men. *Now, if this isn't sexist, I don't know what is!* You know? And I don't care what kind of reasoning you cloak it in, what kind of explanation you give it, that's the basis for it. They're saying women have this incredible power to seduce men. Men are total idiots who can't control themselves. I mean, that's such *garbage*. It's such *nonsense*. So for

those reasons, I could never reconcile feminism and Judaism or feminism and any extremist, fundamentalist religion, 'cause they're all the same.

Alice has seen gender inequality in her Jewish experiences since she was a child. Whereas other respondents have been able to reconcile this through positive feminist Jewish experiences later in life, Alice has not had this opportunity. Her only exposure to the Jewish religion seems to be through her Orthodox brother and his family. Consequently, her Jewish identity is informed by the anger that these experiences have provoked in her. The next chapter shows how other secular Jews, like Jennifer and Alice, might have different views on Judaism, without the feminist critiques described in this chapter.

Chapter Two

SECULAR ADAPTERS

Claiming Compatibility between Jewishness and Feminism

Rhonda describes herself as "allergic to religion." She became disenchanted with God and Judaism because of the Holocaust. Despite this "allergy," Rhonda strongly identifies as a Jew. "I'm antireligious," she told me, "but I'm very Jewish . . . I am very strongly Jewish. Every word out of my mouth is Jewish, practically."

Rhonda does not belong to a synagogue today and remains ambivalent about religious rituals. She loves the melodies of the service yet gets turned off by the text. Although she adamantly rejects the Jewish religion, and religion in general, there are hints that it still has some hold on her. She has, over the years, participated in some progressive forms of Jewish practice, but not without personal struggle. She also expressed regrets about raising her daughter without any institutional Jewish influence, because now her daughter does not identify as Jewish. Rhonda's Jewish upbringing was about "not putting up with oppression." However, when she participated in student protest movements in college, at first she had moments of asking herself, "What's a nice Jewish girl like me doing sitting in a building?" In time, this activism became personally transformative, and she ultimately came to understand how it was rooted in her Jewish rearing.

It may be strange to hear Rhonda say that she is disenchanted with Judaism and yet feels strongly Jewish at the same time. This distinction is not easily measured. By designating herself as more or less Jewish, Rhonda is conveying important information about her own perception of herself as a Jew. It has nothing to do with religiosity, but is an indication of the perceived intensity of one's Jewish identity or the importance of being Jewish relative to others.

While the women discussed in the previous chapter told stories of Jewish-feminist identity negotiation that were rooted in the tensions between traditional Judaism and feminism, this chapter presents a second paradigm for understanding the navigation of Jewish feminist identities. The women discussed here see their Jewish and feminist identities as complementary. In their interviews, they articulated an ideology of cultural Jewishness that is congruent with feminism, which I call the "discourse of Jewish-feminist congruence." This discourse draws parallels between Jewishness and feminism. All of the interviewees explored in this chapter are secular Jews.

SECULAR JEWISH IDENTITY

In contrast to the religious women discussed in chapter one, the women presented in this chapter do not identify with the Jewish religion. They maintain that their Jewish identities are strictly ethnic or cultural rather than religious. They see being a secular Jew as a viable alternative to the Jewish religion. Besides referring to themselves as secular Jews, they also call themselves "cultural Jews," "politically Jewish," or, in the case of one interviewee, a "culinary Jew."

To be a secular Jew is to identify with the Jewish people, culture, ethics, and history more than the Jewish religion.[1] Saul Goodman, in the introduction to his collection of writings by historic secular Jews, writes: "Jewish secularism suggests a philosophy which perceives all that is good and valuable in non-Jewish cultures, but as seen through the prism of Jewish history, which shaped both the Jewish collectivity and the individual Jew."[2] Jewish feminist scholar Laura Levitt sees secular Jewishness as posing a challenge to dominant American models of religion and difference.[3] Yet, as we will explore below, being a secular Jew is actually quite common.[4] The closest parallel in Christianity might be a family whose members celebrate Christmas but never go to church and may or may not believe in God. One might call them "secular Christians." Secular Judaism, however, is more profound than that: it has a long history and deep roots.

Contemporary American discourses of secular Jewishness can be traced back to the *Haskalah* movement, often called the Jewish Enlightenment.

The *Haskalah,* beginning in the eighteenth century in Western Europe and the nineteenth century in Eastern Europe, emerged from the European Enlightenment.[5] In European cities during the Enlightenment, many of the restrictions against Jews were relaxed, and in some cases Jews were granted citizenship and allowed into high schools and universities.[6] The *Maskilim* (members of the *Haskalah* movement) advocated the acculturation of Jews into mainstream societies.

For the first time in Jewish history, peoplehood and religion could be separated.[7] The *Haskalah* resulted in two conceptualizations of cultural membership for Jews. Especially in Western Europe, many Jews saw themselves as citizens of their country who happened to be Jewish by religion. Their national identities were allied with the country, while Jewishness was relegated to faith. The other strand, more prevalent in Eastern Europe, saw itself as Jewish culturally, profoundly tied to the Jewish people, but without the Jewish religion. This group had Jewish national identities that linked them to Jews throughout the world and advocated Yiddish language, literature, theater, and culture. This second ideology is the predecessor of secular Jewish culture in America today.[8]

At the turn from the nineteenth to the twentieth century, many secular and progressive Jewish groups flourished in the United States, including the labor Bundists, Yiddishists, and Zionists. Those groups, formed by Eastern European immigrants, influenced the founding of contemporary organizations of secular Jews. There are secular Jewish institutions in this country today that have been in existence for a century, including *shulas* (afternoon schools that teach Yiddish language and secular Jewish culture) and socialist Jewish camps. They emphasize the transmission of Jewish culture through social justice work, language, food, and cultural expressions such as folk music and dance, plays, and literature.

Three national secular Jewish organizations are the Center for Cultural Judaism, the Society for Humanistic Judaism, and the Congress of Secular Jewish Organizations. The Center for Cultural Judaism (affiliated with the Posen Foundation) supports secular Jewish education and academic research and teaching on secular Jewish life.[9] The Society for Humanistic Judaism was founded in the 1960s by Detroit rabbi Sherwin Wine. Members celebrate Jewish holidays and lifecycle events with "freedom from supernatural authority."[10] The organization's mission includes feminism: "Secular Humanistic Judaism offers a non-theistic approach to Jewish identity and Jewish culture. It also promotes certain important values in Jewish life that the traditional establishments have resisted. These values are rationality, personal autonomy, feminism, the celebration of human strength and power, and the development of a pluralistic world with mutual understanding and cooperation among all religions and philosophies of life." The Congress of Secular Jewish Organizations also refers to social justice in its mission statement: "The Congress of Secular Jewish Organizations (CSJO) is composed of independent organizations that promote a secular expression of its members' Jewish heritage, with particular emphasis on the culture and ethics of the Jewish people. For us the continuity and survival of the Jewish people are paramount. The prophetic tradition of social justice and humanism is the foundation upon which our continuity is built. As Jewish organizations with a secular world view, we stress the historic, cultural, and ethical aspects of our Jewishness in an effort to create identity that is relevant to contemporary life and committed to justice, peace, and community responsibility."[11]

It is possible to be affiliated with Humanistic Judaism or secular Jewish organizations as an alternative to the normative Jewish denominations, such as Reform, Conservative, Reconstructionist, and Orthodox. However, many Jews who identify themselves as secular use the term to mean that they are not affiliated with any Jewish organizations, secular or otherwise. In fact, the women whose stories appear in this chapter did not even seem aware of the existence of Humanistic Judaism, with the exception of Jill, who had attended some meetings of her local chapter. For these women, being secular is an individual identity and connotes lack of involvement in any kind of organized Jewish life; they are completely unaffiliated.

Since Judaism requires action rather than belief, and ritual observance is prioritized over belief in God, it is possible to be a religiously observant Jewish atheist. In contrast to Christianity, which mandates that one must hold a specific set of beliefs to be Christian, there is no essential doctrine dictating what Jews are supposed to believe.[12] The secular-identified women in my sample, however, are atheists and construct their Jewish identities in opposition to the religion.

Contesting one's religion can be seen as a particularly Jewish experience.[13] Challenging Judaism does not make one less Jewish. Feminist scholar Elaine Marks, in an autobiographical essay, expresses the view that nonbelief is Jewish: "I am Jewish precisely because I am not a believer, because I associate from early childhood the courage not to believe with being Jewish; I am Jewish because of familial ties and loyalties; I am Jewish because of the memory, transmitted to me by members of my family, of suffering and pain."[14]

When the respondents in this chapter told me that they were secular, it was usually through statements such as "I connect to the culture rather than the religion," or "Being Jewish is a major part of who I am, but it's an ethnic identity," or "I'm an atheist; I don't like religion." Lisa, who was raised in a Yiddishist family, said, "I'm not a religious Jew; I don't go to temple, and my contact with Judaism is cultural." Jill said, "The religion aspect isn't for me." Evelyn, who became an atheist after she stole some candy as a young child and realized that God did not "strike her down," said, "I am totally a secular Jew and have no interest in the religious aspect."

The root of secularism is in the meaning and motivation applied to one's own Jewish observance. Although many of the people I interviewed claimed to be disconnected from the Jewish religion, virtually everyone engaged in at least some Jewish customs. A secular Jew may observe a few holidays and lifecycle rituals, yet interpret such observance as nonreligious and motivated by cultural ties. Eleanor is married with two grown children. Her description of her family's Jewish observance illustrates this framework: "We've never been involved with any synagogues or anything. We've always celebrated Passover kind of as a Jewish Thanksgiving. And we've always made our own *hagaddah,* which has been kind of, you know, progressive and changes year to year and things like that.[15] Celebrated Chanukah, not much more than that . . . I always take off from work on the Jewish holidays, on Rosh Hashanah and Yom Kippur. And that's more a way of saying that I'm different from other people. It's a cultural diversity issue more than anything else." Being secular is not as much about practice as it is about belief. Eleanor's family may celebrate Passover, but for her it is akin to Thanksgiving, a nonreligious holiday. Eleanor appears to others to be practicing Judaism, but she frames the rituals as secular rather than Jewish observances.

Like Eleanor, the other women discussed in this chapter also do not belong to synagogues. In addition to not connecting to the Jewish religion, some even described themselves as "antireligious." Their antipathy is not toward Judaism in particular but more toward the idea of organized religion in general. Terry, a lesbian feminist musician, expressed her anger vividly: "Religions are man's attempt to control spirituality. And no matter who it is, all fundamentalism is the same, whether it's Jewish fundamentalism, whatever. They're all the same. They're all boys. They're all control. They're all anti-spirit. They're all anti-children. They're all anti-women. They're all anti-life. They're all anti-wholeness. That's what feminism is to me: it's a movement toward wholeness and away from fragmentation;

it's to bring the parts together. That's my spirituality. That's my feminism. That's my Jewishness." Here Terry frames the mission of her spirituality, her feminism, and even her Jewishness as a move toward wholeness. Her use of the phrase "my Jewishness" implies that she has given it her own meaning, or has turned Jewishness into something that she can call her own. Terry creates her own Jewishness as a remedy to male-dominated religions, including Judaism.

Many secular Jews affirm their Jewish identities by virtue of their interest in Jewish topics. Paying attention can be a Jewish behavior: following stories on Jewish subjects in the newspaper, reading about the Holocaust, going to Jewish films, and reading Jewish literature. In this vein, the philosopher Garry M. Brodsky wrote about his own secular Jewish identity: "the differences between me and my non-Jewish colleagues and friends traceable to my Jewishness amount to little more than that I pay more attention to American-Jewish culture and to the Holocaust than they do."[16]

Being Jewish is a nonreligious, non-God-centered identity for the interviewees discussed in this chapter; yet it is unquestionably one of their identities. Jewish identity for these women is about being part of the Jewish people. It is oriented toward the family and home, without the structure of religious customs and institutions. Even though they are all secular, some are more culturally assimilated than others. In other words, there can be a range of intensity of Jewish identities, even for nonreligious Jews. This explains why some of the secular Jews I interviewed mentioned being Jewish only incidentally and said that it is something they do not think much about. On the other hand, others claimed to be very strongly Jewish, even though they are secular.

"COGNITIVE DISSONANCE IS FOR THE RELIGIOUS"

Whereas the narratives in the previous chapter addressed the tensions between Jewishness and feminism, the women discussed in this chapter do not personally relate to the idea of Jewish-feminist dissonance. They see no inconsistency between being Jewish, in their way, and being feminists. They maintain that being both Jewish and feminist does not cause personal conflicts.

Feminism operates in tension with Jewishness through androcentric religious texts, a patriarchal legal structure, male-dominated religious institutions, and exclusion of women from prayer leadership. These constructions of Jewishness are alien to the ways in which secular Jews define their Jewish identities. People without a personal connection to the Jewish religion do not see these issues as relevant to their identities. So when I asked the nine women in this chapter, who are all secular, whether they felt tensions in being Jewish feminists, I was met with a resounding "No."

The idea of Jewish-feminist dissonance was almost incomprehensible to Evelyn, a seventy-something-year-old academic. When I asked her if she ever feels conflict between her Jewish and feminist identities, she initially did not understand the question. So I explained to her that some Jewish feminists feel cognitive dissonance because Judaism is patriarchal, at which point she responded in an exasperated tone: "What religion isn't patriarchal? And what woman identifies with the patriarchal aspects of — ? I mean, religious women, I suppose, do. Religious Jews, I suppose, do. Why are they feminists? I mean, I don't get that . . . I really don't know what they're talking about. Spell it out for me, because I feel stupid on this one. I don't know what they're talking about." Evelyn's bafflement underscores the situated nature of Jewish identity. As a secular Jew who describes herself as antireligious, she cannot grasp the tension that another feminist may feel just from sitting in synagogue and reading a prayer book with male God-language or experiencing the absence of women from the weekly Torah portion. She is so removed from a religious conception of Jewish identity that the meaning of my question was not even apparent to her. She downplays the problematic nature of sexism within Judaism by putting it in the context of other religions.

By attaching the label "religion" to what is sexist in Judaism, the secular Jewish feminist can maintain congruity between her feminist viewpoint and her conception of herself as a Jew. As a result, she is able to escape the conflicts that religious Jewish feminists feel. She relegates the problematic content of Jewishness to religion and thereby diminishes its personal impact.

When I asked Ann, a feminist academic living in the Midwest, whether there has ever been tension for her between her Jewish and feminist identities, she responded: "No. Because the Jewish identity is so minimal and so much based on just what I choose. If I had to observe the rules and customs, then yes." Since her way of being Jewish does not entail proscribed behavior, it does not pose an obstacle to her feminism. She also implies that since being Jewish is a matter of personal choice and is of minimal importance to her, it does not adversely affect her emotions.

Likewise, when I asked Randi, an accomplished writer, whether she was aware when she was younger that Judaism was patriarchal, she replied, "No" and explained: "I don't have a connection with the Bible or with those institutions of Judaism. And when I do, through reading, it doesn't mean very much to me."

Kathie, a doctoral candidate, also said that she does not experience tension between her Jewishness and her feminism, reiterating the nonreligious nature of her Jewish identity: "Oh, no, no. And again, I'm not—I'm interested in Judaism as a religion, but much more culturally. So I don't—it's not a big trigger for me, all this stuff about the paternal, the patriarchal stuff, nature of Judaism. That just isn't where I get triggered . . . for a lot of reasons. I think it's interesting. It just hasn't affected my life in that way, you know." As in Randi's statement above, here the Jewish religion is an intellectual interest rather than a personally meaningful identity. When the patriarchal aspects of Jewishness are located neatly within the category of religion, they become irrelevant to these two women's identities.

Lisa, an activist in the women's peace movement, identified her Jewish upbringing as "Yiddishist." She responded to the question of cognitive dissonance similarly: "Oh, no, because my Judaism isn't directed by the religion. It's directed by the accident of birth and my parents being very consciously Jewish, culturally Jewish. And I think a lot of it is the outsider status, and being a woman is being an outsider." Here Lisa calls on an element of Jewish culture that she feels is compatible with feminism to explain that her Jewish identity does not have to be in conflict with her feminism.

Since the women in this group construct their Jewish identities as separate from the Jewish religion, they are able to balance their Jewishness and their feminism without much apparent ambivalence. When I asked Terry whether she experiences cognitive dissonance between her Jewish and feminist identities, she replied by substituting "lesbian" for "feminist": "Au contraire . . . being a lesbian and being Jewish are very similar . . . To me it's seamless, all of it." When I asked whether patriarchal religion was a trigger for her, she responded, "Fuck it. No. It's *guys*. It's *boys*. Who needs it? Who cares?" Terry rejects the Jewish religion by equating it with masculinity, and through this rejection she claims to be free of personal conflict with Judaism.

FINDING COHERENCE IN BEING JEWISH AND FEMINIST

We have all heard members of ethnic groups say things like "My people always serve massive quantities of food," or "My people are boisterous and argumentative." Just as we construct stereotypes about the other, we also pass on ideas about our own subcultures. Members of a culture collectively construct ideas about what it means to belong to that group. They create those ideas communally through dialogue, literature, and teaching. Such ideas, which I call communal discourses, are not written directly in a text but are formulated over time and passed on from generation to generation. Communal discourses are collectively held ideologies about a group's values and beliefs.

Communal discourses are not universal. The members of the group do not all interpret the values and beliefs of their group in the same way. For instance, Orthodox Jews and secular Jews have very different interpretations of what Judaism is about. Political causes, such as opposing gender, racial, and economic inequality, are not generally seen as key Jewish obligations from the Orthodox perspective. Yet secular Jews, like those described in this chapter, interpret Judaism in a way that makes such social causes primary.

For many of the people in this chapter, social justice is so essential to Judaism that it constitutes the extent of their Jewish "practice." This particular communal discourse of Jewishness is popular among liberal Jews. It allows Jewish activists to feel a deep connection to being Jewish that is compatible with their political perspectives. They are able to translate their activist passions into Jewishly oriented pursuits. Jill, who was active in the feminist theater movement, said, "I'm glad I'm Jewish . . . because I think that being Jewish for me stands for being an activist, and being an aware person in the world, and having a certain sensibility, and understanding oppression, and wanting to help the world be better."

The interviewees quoted in this chapter enunciate a discourse of Jewish-feminist congruence, linking feminism to Jewishness and describing ways in which the two identities are complementary. The discourse of Jewish-feminist congruence contains three common themes. The first, which is related to social justice, is that one's activism, and more specifically one's feminism, is connected to the value of "repairing the world" (*tikkun olam* in Hebrew) in Judaism or a history of progressive activism among American and European Jews. The second theme is that Jewish "otherness" prepares one to intuitively grasp woman's alterity. The third theme, closely related to the second, is that Jews have traditionally held a critical perspective on society because of a history of Talmudic debate, and of questioning authority.[17]

I am interested in these ideas as narratives of identity construction and make no claims about their factuality. What is important for my analysis is not whether it is true that Jews are more likely to be feminists because of a history of marginality, but that Jewish feminists use this idea to construct their relationship to their ethnic group.

These intersections of Jewishness and feminism—social justice, otherness, and questioning—are presented as ways in which the two identities can peacefully coexist. They are often used as a causal explanation for why being a Jew led the teller to being a feminist. Through this discourse of Jewish-feminist congruence, even those who feel alienated from the religion can connect to elements of Jewish culture or universalist values in Judaism. This discourse is a valuation of Jewishness that allows the teller to feel positive about being Jewish.

TIKKUN OLAM: JEWS VALUE SOCIAL JUSTICE

There are many references to *tikkun olam* in Jewish texts, but varying ideas about how to achieve it. Traditionally, the world is seen as broken, and Jews can help perfect it by observing the *mitzvot* (Jewish commandments; the plural of *mitzvah*). Often, there is congruence among the *mitzvot* and the general aims of activists. For instance, many activists care about feeding the hungry, and feeding the hungry is, in fact, one of the 613 *mitzvot* of Judaism. However, fighting for social equality does not necessarily fit the traditional definition of a *mitzvah*. Many of the *mitzvot* are concerned more with personal behavior, such as dietary laws and observance of Sabbath. So the concept of *mitzvot* has taken on a more expansive meaning among today's liberal Jews. The Reform movement of Judaism has emphasized the importance of social justice as a key value of the denomination.

Progressives and others who share a concern for social justice claim that *tikkun olam* signifies social justice. Thus arises the communal discourse that social justice is a prime value of Judaism. Although this is a popular interpretation of Judaism among modern-day liberal Jews, it is only one of many. More socially conservative Jews do not stress social justice as a central tenet of Judaism.

When I interviewed Jennifer, it was clear that she sees the tension between divergent conceptions of Jewish tenets. Jennifer was raised in a Conservative Jewish household before she became a feminist activist and academic. She said that she "abandoned institutional Judaism" when she was a young woman. She became fed up with Jewish men, in particular, after some significant negative experiences with rabbis. Jennifer explained why she remains a Jew despite her animosity toward Jewish community members: "I'm a Jew because I find the ethics absolutely in concert with what I value—that is, the ethics I like, not the ethics I don't . . . But to do justice, to love mercy . . . There's also a thing that says if you're walking down the street and there's a crippled, a lame person ahead of you, it's not nice to pass that person up. You should walk with that person . . . I believe in *tikkun olam*. I believe that the *mitzvot* are worth performing, that they're well-defined." Jennifer is speaking of reinterpreting Jewish values, taking the good and valuing it despite what else is there. This is how multiple and often contradictory discourses of Jewishness are constructed. Jennifer, like perhaps most Jews, freely chooses to identify with some Jewish beliefs and to critique and distance herself from others.

Jennifer enunciates a generalized view of Jewish ethics that underscores the complex and contradictory interpretations of what it means to be a Jew. She uses the Hebrew word *mitzvot* to signify good deeds and ethical behavior. Traditionally, however, this term connotes the rules regulating every aspect of a Jew's behavior, from what one eats to sexual conduct. For instance, an Orthodox Jew has very specific understandings of what the *mitzvot* are, including not touching money on the Sabbath or a man's not touching his wife during her menstrual period. A secular Jew, such as Jennifer, certainly has no intent to observe these more specific, stringent *mitzvot*. She is not alone in using this term creatively, to connote "good deeds" in a very general sense.

Evelyn also uses the term *mitzvah* in this way. "I mean, you see, if you say to me, a Jewish person, I think of some of the things we've talked about. People who, for example, will put something at risk for a principle . . . Jewishness for some significant numbers of us means doing *mitzvahs*, doing good . . . I think it leads to being in the Left, perhaps."

Another interviewee, Kathie, said that she was "thrilled" when she discovered the theme of *tikkun olam* while studying *Kabbalah* (the mystical tradition of Judaism). Kathie claims that she was not proud to be Jewish when she was growing up because of internalized anti-Semitism. She has been learning more about Judaism and working on feeling good about being Jewish. In her recent exploration of Judaism, Kathie has focused on Jewish values that are compatible with her activist values: "So to repair the world, that feels like the core of my identity as a human being. That's my mission, to make a difference to social justice. And so to find that that's part of Jewishness, that's a core piece of Jewishness, and to me that's a core piece of feminism, so there's a natural connection there." Kathie has been a social activist for her entire adulthood. By retroactively connecting her own value of social justice to Judaism, she is forging a coherent Jewish feminist identity as an adult. She has come in contact with the idea of social justice in Judaism in recent years, and it has provided her with a new discourse through which to construct her Jewish identity. It is through reproducing the discourse of Jewish-feminist congruence that Kathie has overcome the negativity she associated with her Jewish identity as a youth.

Rhonda was raised by an Orthodox mother and a secular communist/ socialist father. The socialist-identified interviewees in this sample define socialism as a worldview rather than a political affiliation. For them, to identify as socialist means to dedicate oneself to overcoming class inequality. They might vote for a Democratic president, but they consider themselves socialist because of their perspective on social issues. Rhonda defines Jewishness similarly, as a framework, a lens that focuses on social justice.

Rhonda told me on the phone before we met that she had been obsessing over her Jewish identity her entire life. When I asked her during the interview what it is about being Jewish that inspires her to obsess over it, she answered:

> It's my life! It's who I am . . . It's not a choice. If you take away the Jewishness, I don't know what would be left [laugh].
>
> What is valuable to me is social justice. It's the whole history of social justice. I think being Jewish—this is too instrumental, but—it gives me a lens on the world. It frames the way I understand race relations. It gives me my commitment to fighting against the horrible racism in this society. It is very much combined with the working-class consciousness that I talked about before, which helps me to see, to understand my world, and understand the hypocrisy and the evil in the world.
>
> I don't know . . . it's a framework. It's like feminism, it's like class. It's a framework on the world. It's a mythology.

In other words, for secular progressive activists such as Rhonda, being Jewish entails communal discourses about social inequality. And because feminism is fundamentally about social inequality, this conception of Jewishness fits seamlessly with feminism.

Like Rhonda's father, Ann's father was a communist, and Ann views her "red diaper" upbringing as central to the formation of her feminist consciousness. "Neither of my parents identified strongly as Jewish," she told me, and her father "was very antireligious," although he came from an Orthodox family. Ann remembers growing up with the idea that social justice is important to Judaism, although it was implicitly understood rather than taught directly: "And I did learn from, I guess, my family that there was a connection between the social activism, the concern about justice, that was part of Judaism . . . I don't remember being taught that explicitly, but I grew up in it . . . As a Jew you had the obligation to make the world better." Ann also refers to a history of persecution as a call to action for Jews. "You were exterminated, got through all of this terrible hatred throughout the generations. So you've got to fight against that." She relates being Jewish to being feminist with her view that "being Jewish puts a burden on you to act, and being a feminist puts a burden on you to act."

Some people extend the theme of *tikkun olam* in Jewish liturgy to a perceived history of Jewish activism. This is another collective discourse common among liberal Jews—that Jews have historically been activists and are concerned with pursuing justice in the world at large. Lisa, who was raised in a secular Jewish communist community, recalls growing up with the idealized view of Jews as a utopian people: "I always felt like Bella [Abzug] did in saying that Jews believed in justice.[18] I knew that there were rich Jews and there were poor Jews, and there were strikes against the Jewish garment workers. But basically I thought that Jews were on the side of justice. Sort of a utopian people. It was just what I got out of my childhood. That to be a Jew, you had to be moral. And it was so unbelievably un-analytical, because clearly there were some Jews in government and industry, and all of that, who were the so-called class enemies. But I still believed that Jews were good people." At the same time that Lisa enumerates the communal discourse of Jewish social justice, she deconstructs this discourse and shows that it is merely an ideology.

OTHERNESS AND QUESTIONING

Another theme in the communal discourse of Jewish-feminist congruence goes along with the theme of *tikkun olam*. Jews are said to possess a socially critical standpoint or a special consciousness of injustice in the world. According to this idea, Jewish people are more likely to be activists and progressives or to be concerned with social justice for two reasons. First, the history of marginalization and persecution experienced by Jews has resulted in sensitivity to the plight of others. And second, the encouragement of dissent has been a thread throughout the Jewish tradition.

Barbara, an academic administrator and researcher, is proud to be Jewish because she feels that Judaism values education and intellectualism. She voiced the discourse of Jewish-feminist congruence with the outsider's perspective theme: "I got this insight from a former student of mine who's not Jewish, from Winnetka, Illinois. She believes that Jewish people are more creative in this country, because from the beginning we stand outside the dominant stream. And so we learn to be somewhat critical. We have an outsider's eye." Barbara uses this "insight" that was shared with her by someone else, a non-Jew, to explain why being Jewish and being feminist are compatible perspectives. Ironically, the communal discourse in her case was explicitly voiced by someone outside the community.

Evelyn described feeling ambivalent about her Jewishness. After depicting an interpretation of Jewishness that is aligned with feminism, she offered evidence of the contradictory nature of identities with a statement she made at the end of her interview: "I'm Jewish and I am a feminist, but I don't think the two have much to do with each other." Evelyn grew up poor in the Bronx, raised by her immigrant mother. Being Jewish symbolized deprivation for her, and the anti-Semitism she faced as a kid scarred her. Her participation in the Left dates back to the 1930s.

Evelyn also draws from the discourse of Jewish-feminist congruence. Here she describes the common theme of otherness, connecting Jewish participation in protest movements to Jews' own experiences of oppression: "I think the reason you find so many Jews in the Communist Party, so many Jews in the civil rights movement, so many Jews in feminism . . . was because we already came to the world with a sense, a knowledge, even if we didn't experience it, that anti-Semitism exists. And a sense of the injustice of that, and especially in the post-Hitler era."

Eleanor's Jewish identity seemed to be defined largely by cultural difference; she emphasized the idea that Jews have "outsider status." Eleanor did not receive any formal Jewish training and did not speak very positively about the Jewish community of her suburban New York childhood. Although she defines her Jewishness as cultural rather than religious, she refers to religious texts in relating her Jewish and feminist identities: "I think that what resonated for me in Judaism was resistance to authority or resistance to unjust authority that is in the Passover story. It's in the Chanukah story. It's probably in . . . Esther, you know, and Mordekai and Haman. I think those are the things that stuck with me. Those are the myths or the relevant pictures that I think then resonated with antiwar stuff, feminist stuff." In this passage, she mentions the names of characters from the stories of holidays who subverted the governments of their day to save their people. In other words, the protagonists of these important Jewish stories are heroicized because of their courage to resist tyranny and confront authority. What better influence for radical social action than these stories? What Eleanor's narrative fails to take into account is the many other stories from Jewish tradition involving blind obedience to authority.

Eleanor also referred to the tradition within texts of authors (rabbis) debating ideas, the layering of multiple interpretations that the Talmud comprises. She contrasts an image of Jewish thought to Catholicism: "I think that's another thing about Judaism, you know, which you certainly hear in, like, the *hagaddah,* the questioning of authority. Not just the questioning of authority like the Pharaoh questioning of authority, but the questioning of points, the Talmudic debate about things. As opposed to the Catholic religion that I saw when I was growing up with my friends, where there was the catechism. There was a question and an answer, and that was it. There was a way to do things. Whereas for Jews, there is debate. So I think that played into a lot of the political stuff." In other words, just as feminists and other progressives value debate and dissent, so does the Jewish tradition. Eleanor is constructing her relationship to Judaism by connecting her own political activist history to a Jewish value of questioning.

When I asked her if the previous discussion related to gender for her, she answered: "I think it relates to gender in the sense that the way women were socialized, primarily, when I was growing up was not to question but to be obedient and to do what you were supposed to do. And play into the stereotype. And that perhaps for Jews that was different because of this questioning that came as part of the religion, there was also more of a tendency to question gender roles and the rules, and things like that."

I suspect that Eleanor's discourse is not rooted in her own experience but is drawn directly from cultural ideologies of Jewishness. On the one hand, she divulged the gap between her feminist ideals and her experiences of Jewish women, while on the other, she presented a seamless intersection between Jewish and feminist values. Even though her experience could lead her to doubt the discourse of Jewish-feminist congruence, her interview presents no hint that she feels such doubt. She acts as a vehicle of transmission for a particular interpretation of Jewishness that allows the Jewish feminist to feel in harmony.

Terry was also the daughter of communists, and she herself joined the Communist Party in high school. "I was raised in a very progressive communist household; I was a red diaper baby. So I always had a consciousness, not only about social and economic justice, racial justice, I was raised with all of the movements as part of my life." Terry maintains that her family was not religious because their religion was communism. Instead she was raised "very much as a cultural Jew." Yiddish culture was a big part of her upbringing; her parents sent her to a Yiddish communist summer camp, where she "learned a lot of social history and the unions organizing and social justice and the struggle against Jim Crow and the sweatshops and all that." This "Jewish militant tradition, the nonreligion, the secular Jewish" tradition is still an important part of her identity.

Terry made connections throughout her narrative between her lesbian and Jewish identities, including the quote excerpted in an earlier section of this chapter. She answered many of my questions about the relationship between Jewish and feminist identities by substituting the word "lesbian" for "feminist": "We're not meant to survive. We're outsiders. We're targets. This is one thing that Jews and lesbians have in common. We have an outsider's perspective, which is a great value because mainstream culture is nothing without stealing from all these outsider cultures, the ethnic cultures. And so we have that advantage of that perspective from the outside." Here Terry raises the typical notion of the Jewish outsider's perspective, but instead of linking it to feminism, she connects Jewishness to lesbianism. She interchanges the words "lesbian" and "feminist" as if they were synonymous.

The interview excerpts in this chapter sound more like narratives from focus groups, where research participants talk as a group, bounce ideas off each other, and often appear to be in agreement on key issues. The women here expressed very similar thoughts, yet they are from different communities, places, and age cohorts. Many of the quotes I have excerpted about Jewish-feminist congruence are interchangeable, which reveals how powerful and pervasive collective discourses can be.

Collective discourses are just that—discourses. They are constructed, created by people, ideas that cannot be proved or disproved with reality. Although some collective discourses may be supported with empirical evidence, others cannot be. However, interview narratives often betray the fluid and contradictory nature of discourse. Once an idea is quoted on the page, it appears fixed and real.

One interviewee, in particular, seemed extremely conscious throughout her interview that her identity was taking on a fixed appearance as she spoke. Randi was eloquent in expressing the ambivalences of identity. She was aware that the discourse of Jewish-feminist congruence may be just that, a discourse. She too evoked the "Jew as outsider" theme, yet at the same time she clarified that it does not resonate with her own feelings and experiences. When asked whether she felt a link between being Jewish and being feminist, she replied: "[Pause] Well, both [are] others. I mean, I could spin something for you, but are you asking about my feelings or my experience? Not really, except that they're both outside and, um [pause], but I've always much more strongly felt the gender oppression than the anti-Semitism, much more strongly. I guess because I never felt that Jewish, coming from an American environment. I don't know." This passage, with its pauses, points to the confusion that Randi feels about her Jewish identity. I suppose that this kind of ambivalence is felt by many of the women I interviewed, but Randi is exceptional in that she reflectively remarks on her own confusion throughout the interview. "Spinning" a response, as she puts it, seems to be precisely what the others did when they described the relationship between Jewishness and feminism. Spinning is an apt metaphor for the process in which individuals reinterpret and reiterate communal discourses from their own perspectives.

The discourse of Jewish-feminist congruence contradicts the idea of Jewish-feminist dissonance proclaimed in the previous chapter. However, Jewish culture can be more easily meshed with feminism than the Jewish religion can; thus these secular Jews are more easily able to find compatibility with their Jewish and feminist identities. By constructing a Jewish identity in opposition to a religious framework, each interviewee in this chapter releases herself from the dissonance that other Jewish feminists feel.

The description of Jewish-feminist compatibility is based on cultural discourses of Jewishness among liberal American Jews. Jewish feminists reinterpret images of Jewishness from this cultural discourse to conform to their values. The themes of this discourse are not particular to Jews; they are universal experiences and values. Nonetheless, the tellers reconstruct the themes to imagine a symbiotic relationship between Jewish and feminist identities. The women in this chapter have refashioned Jewishness to fit with their values, and in the process, they offer a counterdiscourse to feminist critiques of Judaism.

Chapter Three

ENCOUNTERING DIFFERENCE

The Search for Belonging
in the Women's Movement

Here is a story about how some fellow students who were not even Jewish taught me more about Jewish identity than all of my reading and research. Picture this: It is the mid-1990s. I am a young graduate student, sitting with the other women in my dissertation group discussing a draft of my latest chapter. I make an offhand comment about how Jews can pass as white, or, more specifically, how Jews who have white skin can pass as non-Jews. Think of your average American Jewish woman walking down the street. Would most people peg her immediately, unquestionably, as Jewish, just by looking at her quickly? No. She would pass as a gentile white woman.

I tell my friends that some Jews are so assimilated that they may go through their whole lives without anyone knowing they are Jewish. I am under the assumption that it is easy in contemporary American culture for Jews to "pass." No, my friends tell me, I am wrong about this one. They argue that I am seeing the issue from the perspective of a Jewish person. In actuality, the world will always label you as a Jew, they tell me, even if you yourself do not. One woman uses the example of a friend who claims to have been raised Jewish but does not identify as a Jew now because he is secular. She tells me that behind his back, all of their mutual friends still think of him as a Jew, even if he claims not to be.

So I am stunned. Here I am, a "Jewish expert," researching and writing about Jewish identity, and yet I had not grasped this simple point: Jews do not blend in completely. Even Jews who have white skin and turn their back on religion cannot shed the Jewish label. They are Jews for life, according to the outside world.

This is a lesson about the limits of self-identification in a world of external labels. Your place in society is impacted by how others perceive you, even if it conflicts with your own identity. For instance, how do American Jews, mostly white and middle-class, fit into American culture? Are they accepted as part of the dominant culture, or do the legacies of anti-Semitism still limit their ability to participate equally? By extension, have Jewish women "passed" in the American feminist movement? Or does being Jewish marginalize them in a movement that has been characterized by racial, class, and sexual divisions?

WHERE ARE THE JEWS IN MULTICULTURAL FEMINISM?

The topic of anti-Semitism raises many conflicting emotions for me. I find myself faced with the same ambivalent feelings that you will see reflected in the interview narratives and writings excerpted below. This ambivalence is common among Jews in contemporary America, who mostly live without any adversity born of anti-Semitism. However, even a basic knowledge of Jewish history prevents me from forgetting that a long string of quiet, safe eras (as in contemporary America) have been sandwiched between many longer, darker periods of persecutions, inquisitions, crusades, and pogroms. Race and class are the major dividing lines in American society; Jews, for the most part, fall on the privileged side of both of those lines. American Jews are not threatened. (Of course, one look at a white supremacist website might give you a different picture.)

My ambiguous feelings have been partly fueled by my experiences in women's studies. Oppression was the main topic of conversation in the classroom, and we were constantly reminded of the need to pay tribute to oppressed groups, remember the intersections of gender with other identities, and understand the relationships between dynamics of oppression. However, I never heard or read the words "Jew," "Jewishness," or "Judaism" in any of my coursework.

I distinctly remember sitting in discussions in my graduate women's studies classes, wondering if being Jewish mattered to my experiences of gender in the same way that Latina women claimed that being Latina mattered to them, or African American women felt that being African American influenced their gender identities. Why did no Jewish women contribute to this discussion about identities and oppression, and why was religion not given consideration as a relevant identity?[1] Was I the only one who noticed this omission? Was I just being too sensitive? Was it selfish of me to want to see Jewish women's voices represented among the multicultural voices of people of color, lesbians, and working-class women? These questions ultimately led to the research project that became this book.

It turns out that I was not the only one asking questions about Jews' place within feminism. Jewish difference was a key theme in my interview accounts. Jennifer said, "I have always been profoundly committed to differentiating myself from the dominant Christian culture . . . I find myself in contrast with much of feminism because of my particular kind of ethnic Judaism." Similarly, Miriam feels that Jewish women should be considered a visible cultural group separate from the appellation "white." She discussed the work of 1970s Jewish feminists as emerging, perhaps unconsciously, from their experiences as Jews in a Christian culture: "If you look at many, I can't say all, of us, but many of the women who were writing and thinking and creating feminism in the seventies, we thought we were writing as women. But we were really writing from the position of Jewish women whose sexuality and sense of self and sense of exploration and sense of being in the world was stifled in WASP culture." Miriam is contending that many Jewish second-wave feminists in the 1970s were mistaken in thinking that their Jewish identities were not relevant. She claims that although they may not have realized it, these women were outside the mainstream, different from non-Jewish women. Their experiences and their perceptions were shaped by being Jewish, just as the expressions of women of color are closely related to their racial identities. Miriam is aware that this point of view goes against the typical exclusion of Jews from multicultural curricula.

The women's liberation movement was initially intended to unite women in sisterhood. Because of the emphasis on building the identity of "woman," differences among women were glossed over. The early second-wave feminist movement was busy examining "woman" as a category of its own, with its own concerns, experiences, and identities. This early women's movement was later criticized for downplaying differences among women and, in doing so, generalizing its ideas and agenda based on white middle-class straight women's experiences. During that stage, American Jewish feminists felt they blended into this category. It is not until they look back that they realize they may not have noticed the Jewish marginalization or anti-Semitism that was occurring in their environment.

UNNOTICED DIFFERENCES

Ambivalence toward one's cultural background—especially Jewishness—is not new, and it has very specific roots. There are many factors that contributed to the way Jews encountered their differences within the women's liberation movement. For Jewish second-wave feminists, the uncertainties around anti-Semitism and feelings about Jews' position in America have been shaped partly by their families' immigration history. Most of them are the children and grandchildren of immigrants who were concerned about assimilating into middle-class America.

Their ideas about Jews' place in the United States were also shaped by their generational cohort. When they were growing up in the 1950s, America was considered a melting pot where diverse ethnic groups were supposed to blend in with the dominant culture. Later, in the 1960s and 1970s, cultural difference and minority pride were celebrated. For the first time in the U.S., minority group assimilation became questioned and diversity honored.

Since in many ways the women's movement of the 1960s and 1970s branched off from other social protest movements of the previous two decades, it is important to look at the Jewish identities of Jewish activists beginning in the 1950s. The feminists I interviewed took part in other social movements both prior to and during their participation in the women's liberation movement. They were members of the civil rights, antiwar, free speech, and labor movements. Some were "red diaper babies" raised by communist or socialist parents or joined socialist study groups in college and graduate school. They used labels such as "radical," "progressive," and "liberal" to define themselves. Their feminist activism was a natural extension of their participation in other social protest movements of the time. Feminism was not the sole political identity for most of the people I interviewed, but rather was one of the many ways in which they mobilized against the problems they witnessed in society.

It is well known that Jews played a large role in the social protest movements of the time. In his book *The Jewish 1960s,* Michael Staub claims that "no other decade during the twentieth century has been so strongly defined by Jewish-led and Jewish-sponsored social activism or so deeply informed and influenced by Jewish culture."[2] For many of the activists I interviewed, however, Jewishness was not an overtly discussed aspect of their activism. In fact, a number of them recalled that being Jewish was not discussed much in the movement and that their own Jewish identities were most submerged at that point in their lives. They describe being less "conscious" of Jewishness during those years—not that they stopped identifying as Jews, but that it did not feel as relevant to their lives. This has been attributed to both the political nature of the time and the negative feelings about religion among the Left.

As an example of the silences around Jewishness in the women's liberation movement, consider a typical activity for feminists of the time: attending consciousness-raising groups. These groups were meant to address everything about the lives of the women who attended them. The group members developed strong, intimate bonds with each other. Yet the women I spoke with could not recall whether there were other Jews in their groups or whether Jewishness even entered into their discussions. This absence did not seem to be an issue of faulty memory, but rather was reflective of the silences in their experiences.

When I asked interviewees whether they were aware of how many of the women in their consciousness-raising groups were Jewish, here are some of the responses I received:

LISA: It wasn't like my top priority [to be aware of who was Jewish].

JILL: One other person may have been Jewish. I don't know that, though. Jewish had nothing to do with it. Nothing came up about being Jewish at all . . . or did it?

KATHIE: So, I mean, we knew each other was Jewish. It was not something we talked about, it wasn't that we hid, but it wasn't like a conscious bond . . . You know, the Jewishness wasn't something that we talked about or cared about that much. It just was.

I felt that asking informants how many Jews had been in their consciousness-raising groups was a valid question. However, some of their responses seem to carry an undertone of defensiveness, as if my question was ridiculous. We can conclude from the comments above that the role of Jews in the movement was not a conscious issue for many feminists during the women's liberation movement. However, this chapter will demonstrate that many of the women I interviewed became concerned with this issue later in their lives.

I thought that my question about how many Jews were in a consciousness-raising group might provide some sort of historical picture of Jewish involvement in the women's movement, or at least in consciousness-raising groups, or at least within feminist networks. I did not expect respondents to be so baffled by it. For me, the answer to such a question would have been easy to recall. However, awareness of who around you is Jewish might be related to how strong your own Jewish identity is, or how much you are up front about being Jewish yourself.

I was surprised that some of my informants had no idea which of their friends and fellow activists were Jewish because that is something that I have always been so aware of myself. I must confess that when I look back at my kindergarten yearbook, I can easily pick out the Jewish children. Not from their names or the way they look, but because I distinctly remember that much about each person. I guess it was important to me to know who, like me, was Jewish. That is all I remember about the children pictured because I changed schools in first grade and may not have seen them again. Yet when I look at those faces from thirty years ago, I am absolutely certain who is a Jew and who is not.

I often refer to this ability to identify other Jews as "Jewdar" (à la "gaydar" for gays and lesbians). Much is revealed by the fact that some of the women I interviewed were completely oblivious about who was Jewish in their close feminist circles, and that being Jewish was not a subject broached in consciousness-raising groups when the intimate details of participants' lives were being discussed. It points to the extent of Jewish invisibility within the women's liberation movement. Put simply, being Jewish was just not relevant.

THE CLOAK OF INVISIBILITY EXPANDED: JEWS IN THE LEFT

When I interviewed Rhonda, a Marxist-identified academic, she expanded upon the idea of Jewish invisibility within feminism by claiming that it is a phenomenon within the Left more generally. She had recently been conducting research in the area of Jewish studies, and her dissertation was about Jews as well: "Even going into anti-Semitism more came from doing this research . . . I realized how much I had suppressed. And I think that partly growing up . . . and living in a kind of leftist milieu in the late sixties did not encourage looking at anything about Jewishness. And in fact when I decided to do the dissertation that I did, I didn't get a lot of encouragement from my leftist friends, because they didn't see Jews as an oppressed group or an interesting group in any kind of way. And I think the fact that I taught about ethnic groups and racial inequality for so many years, without dealing with anti-Semitism, speaks volumes." Rhonda attributes her own avoidance of teaching about anti-Semitism to a prevalent attitude among the Left: Jews are not oppressed, so there is no reason to study them. Jewishness is a topic about which many leftists (Jews included) feel ambivalent, and thus it has remained a largely unspoken, uninvestigated, and imperceptible category of analysis.

There are many reasons for this invisibility of Jews in the 1960s Left. For one, religion was considered passé. Young activists were rebelling against "the establishment"—meaning any institutional authority structure—and certainly against old dogma. Religion was considered a prime example of what they rejected in society. Although ethnic and cultural differences were beginning to be celebrated, Jews were considered by many to be a religious category rather than an ethnic group. Given the antipathy toward religion in activist communities, Jews did not feel encouraged to embrace their Jewishness in any way during this time period.

One interviewee, Kathie, a lesbian feminist who had recently been exploring Judaism, recalled that during her radical activist years in the sixties and seventies, she would never have marched for a Jewish cause: "But I would march for every issue except the Jewish issue. I mean, if that would have come up, I would have felt disgust and disdain, like—why would you ever march for that? And here I was out there on the street, for not everything, but a broad array of social issues . . . I think on the Left there was this unconscious, you know—and a lot of leaders were Jews, but it wasn't talked about and there was not a value about valuing it. And I bought right into that . . . That's a big thing, the discounting of Jewish oppression." Kathie attributes this refusal to take up Jewish issues to her own history of internalized anti-Semitism. She also feels that other Jewish activists' experiences were characterized by internalized anti-Semitism and that anti-Semitism was present among the Left more generally.[3]

Another issue that influenced the downplaying of Jewishness in the Left was Jewish activists' relationship to the American assimilation process. Young Jews in the 1960s, who had grown up as either the children or grandchildren of immigrants, were eager to assimilate into the American mainstream. In the 1950s, their families were striving to fit into middle-class American culture. American Jewish culture at the time of their upbringing was focused on assimilation and Americanization.

American Jews reached the height of their success in the post–World War II years. Many Jews changed their Jewish-sounding last names to circumvent the quotas that commonly restricted the numbers of Jewish students admitted to elite American universities. It was also common to hide one's Jewishness when buying a home. Real estate brokers used a strategy called "redlining"—in which they literally used a red pen to block out certain neighborhoods on a map—to prevent Jews, African Americans, and others from buying homes. Country clubs and other symbols of the American bourgeoisie banned Jews from joining. Affluent Jews of the period who wanted to assimilate were required to downplay their religious difference, their immigrant past, and their ethnic cultural distinction. This trend toward shedding markers of Jewish identity was prevalent among the cohort that included parents of 1960s activists.

A generation later, when Jewish activists heard their fellow activists railing against the "bourgeoisie," it reminded them of their parents—and it reminded them of themselves, too. Jewish and middle-class had become inseparable categories. Even though not all Jews in this country were middle-class, somehow Jews had come to symbolize the nouveau riche. For these activists, the mantra was "You're either part of the problem or part of the solution." As young Jewish activists tried to become part of the solution, they saw their Jewishness as part of the problem: something to give up in the name of justice. It was incredibly easy to put down one's religious and ethnic past—that's what the previous generation had been practicing all along, through assimilation. Unfortunately, this entire generation of Jewish activists helped to lay the foundation for a form of anti-Semitism that was unique to the Left.

Were there Jewish activists—in the feminist movement and other movements—who were proud of their Jewishness and did not try to denigrate it? Sure. But they appear to have been drowned out by the voices of those who became ardently secular, antireligious, or perhaps even anti-Semitic.

ANTI-SEMITISM IN THE AMERICAN FEMINIST MOVEMENT

Anti-Semitism in the American feminist movement has taken many forms. It has been perpetuated through stereotyping, interpersonal conflicts, and the discounting of Jewish oppression itself. It can be obvious and explicit, or more implicit and harder to detect. It has had the effect of either silencing Jewish feminists or motivating them to be more outspoken in proclaiming their Jewishness with pride.

The scholar Rosa María Pegueros has written about her view of anti-Semitism in the feminist movement: "There is amorphous anti-Semitism among some activists of the Left and women's movements . . . Most know nothing about Jewish history; they ignore more than two millennia of anti-Semitism and persecution of the Jews, preferring to conflate all of it into the Holocaust. Willful ignorance is coupled with an unconscious hatred of Jews."[4] Likewise, Evelyn Torton Beck, in the introductory essay to *Nice Jewish Girls: A Lesbian Anthology*, says that "anti-Semitism has been supported by the lesbian-feminist movement (even if out of ignorance and insensitivity)."[5] Beck claims that anti-Semitism often occurs through the denial of Jewish oppression, and she details how some feminist authors, critics, and speakers have not accounted for their own and others' anti-Semitism.

A third scholar, Irena Klepfisz, also discusses the phenomenon of underestimating the historic existence of Jewish oppression: "The anti-Semitism with which I am immediately concerned, and which I find most threatening, does not take the form of the overt, undeniably inexcusable painted swastika on a Jewish gravestone or on a synagogue wall. Instead, it is elusive and difficult to pinpoint, for it is the anti-Semitism either of omission or one which trivializes the Jewish experience and Jewish oppression . . . Even when confronted with these attitudes, the lesbian/feminist response is most likely to be an evasion, a refusal to acknowledge their implications."[6] Klepfisz claims that many Jewish feminists have responded by staying silent about their Jewishness, and when they are in the spotlight, they are afraid to draw attention to it: "For these women, the number of Jews active in the movement is not a source of pride, but rather a source of embarrassment, something to be played down, something to be minimized."[7] Klepfisz attributes this self-silencing of Jewish feminists to internalized anti-Semitism.

MINIMIZING JEWISH OPPRESSION

Rhonda also spoke about the delegitimizing of Jewish oppression within the feminist movement: "The anti-Semitism I have confronted are the assumptions that Jews are all middle-class, that Jews are all wealthy. I have encountered that among feminists who aren't Jewish—'Why do you worry about anti-Semitism after all?' I haven't liked it."

The denial of Jewish oppression occurs within the context of a complicated situation for American Jews, who find themselves in a position of both privilege and marginalization. Jews are mostly white and middle-class in this country and are perceived as being part of the powers-that-be. However, the women discussed in this book feel that this perception contains its own sort of anti-Semitic character. Because of ideas about

Jewish class privilege, non-Jewish feminists have been resistant to Jewish feminist concerns about anti-Semitism.

Despite a long history of oppression throughout many eras and geographical locations, there is scant awareness of Jews as an othered group, worthy of inclusion in the plethora of feminist conferences and publications about cultural identities and oppression. In the 1970s women's liberation movement, Jews were largely silent and invisible, and in the multicultural feminist debates of the 1980s and 1990s, Jewish oppression was rarely seen as a legitimate concern. Instead, it has often been considered inappropriate to include Jews in the long list of marginalized groups.

As the next stories recounted in this chapter will demonstrate, Jewish women sometimes clash with women of color over the idea of oppression. When Jewish feminists claim their Jewishness as an identity that differentiates them from American hegemony, they are occasionally met with anger from feminists of color. The discussion too often turns into a fruitless competition over whose group has historically been persecuted more.

Rosa María Pegueros writes about her experience as one of the few Jews participating in a discussion on an e-mail list of contributors to a well-known anthology of writings by feminists of color. A reference to her experience of anti-Semitism outside of that community was met with hostility from a co-contributor who voiced the concern that the list would become "another place where Jewishness is reduced to a site of oppression and victimization, rather than a complex site of both oppression and privilege."[8] Pegueros was shocked and dismayed when not only did the other contributors decline to speak out in her defense, but several women immediately wrote to support her attacker and "empathized with [the attacker's] concern that the list was becoming a forum for Jews."[9] Apparently, although the group was dedicated to building bridges among diverse feminists, Jews were not central to that aim.

Pegueros notes that a few Jews wrote to the list admitting that they were Jewish in an almost apologetic tone. She writes further about observing something similar among other Jewish progressives, what seems like shame or reluctance to "come out" as Jews. Steven, one of the profeminist men I interviewed, talked about this same issue of ambivalence regarding being "out" about Jewish issues: "There's been some of that in the women's community, too, around feminism . . . If you're raising issues of anti-Semitism, you're taking away from the focus on feminism. So it creates a tremendous amount of ambivalence, I think, in many Jews about just how public and visible to be."

Racism and certain other forms of oppression have been taken on as part and parcel of the feminist cause. Syllabi of women's studies courses must now assign readings on the intersections of gender, class, race, and sexual orientation. Feminist organizations now include in their mandates a commitment to fighting racism, homophobia, and other forms of oppression.[10] Yet anti-Semitism is still not typically part of the discourse on oppression within feminism. I noticed the absence of Jewish women's voices in the multicultural environment of my women's studies education in graduate school. My curiosity about Jewish feminists' identities was awakened by the silence around Jewish identity in everything I read about cultural identity during that time.

Nancy Miller writes about the invisibility of Jews in women's studies and the process of realizing her own silence about her Jewish identity:

> At a feminist conference in 1985, Evelyn Torton Beck, speaking as a Jew and as a feminist, dramatically challenged the feminists in the audience who were Jewish to "take back their noses and their names." When were we going to assume our identity and our responsibility to it? In women's studies curricula every minority or ethnic literature was taught except Jewish. Why, she wanted to know, no courses on women's Jewish-American or Yiddish literature? Beck's challenge was never answered on its own terms because it was immediately displaced into a violent exchange with another panelist, who argued that Jewish women could not consider themselves oppressed, since they could choose to pass, whereas black women did not have this luxury. Jewish women's writing did not belong to the alternative history, the history of the oppressed. I was profoundly disturbed by this debate, not only because it was ugly and classically divisive, but because it forced me to consider why I, a great partisan of "identity," had never thought to assert a Jewish or a Jewish feminist one.[11]

For Miller, both experiences, hearing Beck's challenge and seeing the conflicts within the women's movement around anti-Semitism, served as catalysts. Before that point, she had been completely unaware of her complicity in the silencing of Jewish women. Miller writes that after this conference experience, she began adding Jewish women's writing to her introduction to women's studies courses.

Like Miller, my interviewees expressed dismay at the exclusion of Jews from the academic feminist vision of cultural diversity. Rhonda has been teaching about minority groups and racism in her women's studies and sociology classes for years. When I asked her if she thinks that Jews have a place in the conversation about difference started by feminists of color, she replied: "Well, yeah, I do. It bothers me when there's an anthology and there isn't any kind of a Jewish entry."

Olivia experienced a shift in her Jewish identity after feeling marginalized as a Jew. Olivia is an academic and has been affiliated with ethnic studies fields as well as women's studies. She spoke of having an "Afrocentric identity" that served as a substitute in some ways for her Jewish identity. This identification changed when anti-Semitic speakers were invited to her campus by the African American Studies Department and the black students' organization. The shock and hurt she felt caused her to withdraw from the ethnic studies department at her school and from some of her scholarly community. She began to consider the importance of her own Jewishness more seriously and to assert her Jewish identity more. Anti-Semitism is a theme that runs through Olivia's interview. She feels that an anti-Semitic thread has appeared in ethnic women's literature in recent years. She is also angry that Jews are grouped together with whites; she does not identify as white (although she is of Ashkenazi descent) and feels that this categorization of Jews shows an ignorance of Jewish history.

Sarah, who is an observant Jew, recalled noticing the invisibility of Jews during her participation in a feminist organization back in the 1970s. The organization is still in existence today: "Self-determination of peoples, nobody was interested in that from the point of view of being Jewish. There were lots of Jews in the organization, but—the concept of Jews as a people just as African Americans were seen as a people with a distinctive culture, and different kinds of Latinos were seen as peoples with a distinctive culture, and different kinds of Native Americans were seen as peoples with a distinctive culture—that recognition of the need for that among Jews and the validity of that for Jews wasn't there." This statement suggests that Jews are invisible not only in multicultural feminist discourses, but also in academia and within feminist organizations.

ASSERTING JEWISHNESS

How have Jews in the women's movement responded to this silencing and marginalization? Although some Jewish feminists have internalized the anti-Semitism and kept quiet about their Jewishness, others (like Nancy Miller and Olivia) have been impelled to identify more strongly and visibly as Jews after experiencing anti-Semitism within the feminist movement.[12] As is evident from autobiographical writings and the life stories of my interviewees, although Jewishness was not salient to many Jewish second-wave feminists during their early activist years, it has become more important to them in recent years, partly in response to their exposure to anti-Semitism. "After the shock of coming face to face with anti-Semitism within the international women's movement," Miriyam Glazer writes, "feminists who had been only incidentally Jews were driven to look again at their Jewishness."[13]

Jennifer explained how this process of Jewish awakening might have occurred among feminists of her generation. After she shared with me her experience of encountering anti-Semitism at a women's studies conference in the 1980s, I asked her whether anything similar had happened in the second-wave days. "During the sixties and the seventies? Yeah, but we didn't know it. We didn't recognize it." When I asked why it was more recognizable later on, she responded, "Because we learned more. We thought more. We compared experiences. We understand the dynamics of oppression better. We are less self-hating. We are more realistic about the fact that we are who we are and that we can't become leaders, culturally leaders."

Other narratives about anti-Semitism in the women's movement were framed through a retrospective lens. It was typical for my informants to comment that they had not realized until later that anti-Semitism was at the root of their conflicts with other feminists. Only when they took a look back at the interpersonal alienation they experienced during feminist activism did they realize that their Jewishness was almost certainly the cause.

When Jennifer compared her experiences in the women's movement with those of other Jewish women, she discovered that anti-Semitism was widespread. "Anti-Semitism in the women's movement—I mean, it was here and there—but I had not recognized that it was pervasive. I didn't know that my experiences were being replicated." Her realization reminds me of the classic "aha!" moment, or click moment, that some feminists experienced at consciousness-raising groups. Through discussing their own lives with other women, everything would start to make sense. They would make the connection between their personal lives and other women's experiences, becoming politicized in the process.

Miriam also looked at her past as a time when she did not see the anti-Semitism she was experiencing. She participated in disparate feminist communities, including a separatist rural settlement and women's studies communities, both places where she felt she was treated with hostility because she was Jewish: "But there was definitely some anti-Semitism in the sense that the women from Iowa thought I didn't have any feel for the land. Like Jews are . . . you know, I wasn't a farmer. You know what she was referring to, we're the pariahs . . . I would become the focus of negativity, and it would be anti-Semitism but I wouldn't really understand it."

INTERPERSONAL TENSIONS

I was once asked to participate in a women's studies conference panel about Jewish women's personal styles. The proposal for the panel assumed a common perception of Jewish women as loud, frank, expressive, and generally colorful characters. As a sociologist, I have to question and even doubt generalizations about ethnic personality types. Yet, such stereotypes of Jewish women do exist, and many of the women I interviewed seem to believe them.

For instance, Terry, a lesbian feminist musician, refers to herself as outspoken and claims that "the East Coast Jewish/Italian in-your-face style was unpalatable to a lot of lesbian feminists. They didn't like that I spoke about things that many women were afraid to think of. And I spoke right out about them." Terry is not alone in conflating what she sees as a Jewish woman's style with other ethnic groups such as Italians. In this self-concept, Jewish women perceive themselves as possessing an assertive demeanor that differentiates them from supposedly meeker, more demure WASP women or mainstream models of femininity.

Another secular Jew, Jennifer, described herself in similar terms: "And, you know, I'm fat, I'm loud. I'm what a lot of people are uncomfortable around; if they aren't charmed by me, they're repulsed by me. All that's Jewish about me or ethnic about me, it could be Italian or Greek, but all of that stuff makes a lot of people uncomfortable. But I didn't know that this wasn't only my experience and that skinny Jewish women were having the same problems." In other words, according to Jennifer, Jewish women of many different styles and personas are often perceived as the other by non-Jewish feminists.

Jewish marginalization occurring at the level of interpersonal interactions was a common theme in the interviews I conducted. Some of the women I spoke with felt they were disliked by other feminists because they were Jewish. They described feeling like an outsider within their immediate community, in contrast to other accounts of anti-Semitism that are at the level of broader political debates. "There's blatant anti-Semitism," said Miriam, "and then there's like when people just don't like you for some reason, and it turns out it's the Jewish thing they don't like you for. The things about Jews and money will come out. And I have a few particular very hurtful experiences in the women's community." Others felt that their ethnically Jewish personality styles were not understood by non-Jewish feminists in their networks.

There were other examples of interpersonal conflicts that were seen as arising from the so-called Jewish style of the teller. Jennifer recounted times when Jewish women were verbally attacked at feminist conferences, which she attributed to their obviously Jewish personas. She also told me about the pain she experienced when she was unknowingly ousted from a consciousness-raising group. She was told the group had been canceled when the truth was that the other women wanted her out and chose not to confront her about it.

Jennifer interprets this rejection by her peers as due to her Jewishness: "All [these] Protestant, very WASPy women had gotten together and decided that my personal style was offensive to them. I was too passionate. I was too articulate. I was too analytical. I was too Jewish." She later found out, when meeting with a group of Jewish feminists, that many other Jewish women had experienced similar things. After that meeting, Jennifer decided that anti-Semitism was pervasive in the women's movement, and this knowledge affected her Jewish identity: "And it was at that point that my [sigh] feelings that I had to become more consciously assertive about my Jewish identity began to take fire."

Rachel lived in Texas during the women's liberation movement, after having grown up in big cities in the Northeast and Midwest. She describes this period of her life as full of emotional turmoil. She generally felt like a social misfit and thought her feminist sisters reacted to her differently because she was a Jew: "I was frequently accused of being the most negative person anybody had ever met and also the most hyper, probably because I was the only damn Yankee Jew any of them had ever met . . . And so I was living at three or four times the speed of all the Texans . . . That was just my natural culture . . . I was so used to feeling out of step with everybody. It was just one more feeling out of step. It took me years to sort out that 'damn Yankee Jew' was really a category that made me out of step in particular ways." After that experience, Rachel became more committed to finding a Jewish community in Texas and started attending synagogue services. Since then, she has become a religiously active Jew and a leader in various synagogues.

ANTI-SEMITISM IN THE INTERNATIONAL WOMEN'S MOVEMENT

Jews' place in international feminist dialogues goes beyond the issues presented thus far about the American feminist movement. The major themes evoked in discussions of the movement were questioned oppression, multiculturalism, and personality clashes. However, American feminists attending international women's conferences were forced to consider their Jewish identities beyond U.S. borders and to confront their feelings about Israel as they found themselves tied to a controversial and often hated symbol of international Jewry.

Many of my interviewees mentioned witnessing anti-Semitism at a United Nations International Conference on Women. Some of the reports of anti-Semitism in my interviews and in articles written following the conferences are about hearing hateful speech and anti-Semitic slurs. Other reports relate to official conference resolutions and discussions of the Israeli-Palestinian question. There has been debate about whether the contested rhetoric at the conferences was anti-Israel or anti-Semitic in nature. While some people maintain the important distinction between being anti-Semitic and protesting Israeli policy, others, such as feminist Letty Cottin Pogrebin, argue that the difference between the two is not always clear: "Now that it is open season for attacks on Israel, such criticism, often under the rubric of 'anti-Zionism,' is sometimes a politically 'respectable' cover for anti-Semitism."[14]

The first UN International Conference on Women celebrated the UN Decade for Women in Mexico City in 1975. The Mexico City conference adopted a resolution that called for "the elimination of colonialism and neo-colonialism, foreign occupation, Zionism, apartheid, racial discrimination in all its forms."[15] Although Zionism was conceived as a liberation movement for the Jewish people, it was now being associated with international movements of oppression and racism. Jewish feminists who attended the conference reported that the PLO monopolized and sidetracked the proceedings to focus on the Israeli occupation.[16]

Antagonism toward Zionism continued. Five years later, at the 1980 conference in Copenhagen, the notorious Zionism-equals-racism resolution passed by a vote of 94–4. The four dissenting countries were the United States, Canada, Australia, and Israel.[17] This conference marked the end of the UN Decade for Women. Once again, the Israeli-Palestinian conflict created disagreement among the feminists in attendance. There are conflicting reports about who was intimidating whom and whether the PLO "derailed the conference." Jewish women were highly disturbed by the Copenhagen conference, during which they witnessed anti-Semitic verbal outbursts and censorship of Jewish women speakers.[18] Some attendees at the external conference of NGOs, called the Forum, felt that it was "rigged" by the PLO and that women's issues were sidestepped by the Palestinian issue.

Many Jewish feminists saw the UN conferences as a wakeup call about the existence of anti-Semitism in the international women's movement. In the months after Copenhagen, a group of feminist Jews began meeting to discuss their experiences with anti-Semitism, both in general and specifically within the women's movement. They eventually formed a group called Feminists against Anti-Semitism, which defined itself as both Zionist and feminist, and put anti-Semitism on the agenda of the 1981 National Women's Studies Association (NWSA) conference "Women Respond to Racism."[19]

Naomi was one of the women who helped organize this group. She told me about the resistance she encountered from the NWSA when she and others wanted to conduct a panel on anti-Semitism at their annual conference in Storrs, Connecticut. She responded angrily: "I said, 'Then we're gonna march from New York to Storrs, Connecticut!' They gave us a small room. I said, 'We'll take it.' We were very strong. And not only did we have a panel that was, I can't tell you how packed it was. Because it was at that prickly, prickly high five years after Mexico, the Mexican meeting."

Naomi was inspired to raise awareness about anti-Semitism in the women's movement after attending a few of the early UN International Conferences on Women. Nonetheless, this did not stop her from attending later conferences. She unequivocally described the 1980 Copenhagen conference as "a very anti-Semitic meeting." She also described her experience at a UN meeting in Oslo, "where I met staff people who were virulently anti-Semitic. My breath was taken away."

Another interviewee, Rebecca, a feminist academic, attended the 1995 UN Conference on Women in Beijing. She recalled that the Israeli women at the conference had decided to keep a "low profile" because of the strife at previous UN women's conferences. Rebecca wore a button at this conference that identified her as a Jew. She wanted to show solidarity with other Jewish women, and Israeli women in particular. Here is her memory of the conferences: "It was around the time that within feminism there was a lot of tension over the Arab-Israeli conflict. And there was a distinct almost, well, distinct anti-Israel—that then almost began to have the feeling of an anti-Semitic—tension in feminism. I remember talking to somebody about it in Israel who had been to the Copenhagen UN conference and talking about how the issue became very divisive and very problematic for the Jewish women who were there, particularly the Israeli women who were there . . . And when I went to Beijing, it was as an American but also as a Jew." Rebecca recalls attending a Shabbat service at the Beijing conference, something that she would not typically do. She has occasionally been critical of Israeli policy toward Palestinians. Nonetheless, as a Jewish feminist, she felt the need to show solidarity with Israeli Jewish women. Her vignette supports the idea held by many Jews that anti-Israel sentiment cannot be separated from anti-Semitic sentiment.

AMBIVALENCE ABOUT ISRAEL

Others I spoke to made a point of distinguishing between anti-Semitism and anti-Zionism or opposition to Israeli policy. Also, some of the women did not agree with the Jewish feminists who perceived an atmosphere of anti-Semitism at the conferences. Lisa, who grew up in a secular Jewish communist community, had a different perspective on the UN conferences, but then encountered anti-Semitic and anti-Israeli sentiments at another conference:

> In Copenhagen, I was there. When Letty [Cottin Pogrebin] called me because she was writing an article, and she said, "What about the anti-Semitism there?" and I said, "I didn't feel any anti-Semitism, I felt it was anti-Israel." She didn't quote me . . . And so it was a very troubled conference. But I still didn't think it was about anti-Semitism.
>
> But then I had a terrible experience. I was chairing a panel for Women's Studies International. I've always been involved. There was a wonderful Israeli woman on my panel. When she got up to speak, people got up and walked out! And there was so much anti-Israel and anti-Jewish carrying-on. So I got involved a lot in Jewish issues there. That was really my first time.

For Lisa, as for others, the shock of witnessing anti-Semitism in the women's movement served as a catalyst for getting involved in Jewish issues. It is clear that many American feminists feel a strong tie to Israel and would agree with the concept "Kal Yisrael Arevim Zebazeh": All of Israel is responsible for each other.[20] In other words, Jews are integrally connected around the world, whether in Israel or in diaspora. No matter how critical one is of Israeli policy, when Israel is attacked, Jewish loyalty often takes precedence.

The Israeli occupation was certainly a source of confusion for some Jewish feminists. It took the opposition to Israeli policy voiced by the Left for some of these women to realize what was going on in Israel. Lisa, a long-time member of the women's peace movement, faced personal conflicts when the movement took a stand against Israel:

In Women's Strike for Peace, there were a lot of non-Jews. They were all very with the '67 war. It created problems. Women's International League for Peace came out against Israel, an uncomfortable feeling. That made me uncomfortable. And that was not with feminism, my own personal feeling of discomfort. That was with the peace movement.

Then I was at an antiwar international conference. A Christian man was attracted to me and asked me to go to dinner. He was talking about the '67 war and I had to leave. I just couldn't take it. I couldn't stand knowing the Jews could do that. I wasn't sure I believed it. But I also felt there was some anti-Semitism.

And then I would get very uncomfortable when people I loved condemned Israel. I had a feeling I would have done the same thing. It was very difficult; the whole Israel question raised problems between being Jewish and being feminist.

The downside of "Kal Yisrael Arevim Zebazeh" is feeling culpable for what other Jews do around the globe, even when you do not agree with their actions. Israeli politics has certainly created feelings of ambivalence among American Jewish feminists as well as conflicts between them. Rhonda encountered this conflict while conducting a research project and in her activist work:

I had gotten involved in Jewish activities on the Lebanon war. And in doing that kind of work, I kept running up against people who would say that anybody who criticizes Israel is being anti-Semitic. And that Jews who criticized Israel were self-hating. And that really upset me.

I wanted to deal with this charge that it was anti-Semitic or self-hating to be critical of Israel in respect to Palestinians. It was also just before Letty Pogrebin's article came out about anti-Semitism in which she makes essentially the same charge. And so I had gotten into a huge conflict in my family about Israel and anti-Semitism. And here was a way of exploring the relationship between anti-Semitism and the Palestinian question. That's how I got interested in [my research project].

It is not surprising that Rhonda's outspoken politics engendered controversy within her Jewish family. Israel and anti-Semitism are touchy subjects for American Jews. It is no wonder that perceptions of anti-Semitism in the women's movement and feelings about the Israeli-Palestinian conflict are controversial among Jewish feminists.

As the narratives in this chapter and some of the narratives in the previous chapter suggest, the women I interviewed are apt to view both gender and Jewishness within a framework of marginalization and oppression. This framework is a ubiquitous analytical lens for second-wave feminists, and recent feminist theorists have begun to challenge the sometimes simplistic worldview that results from dualistic paradigms of oppression and victimization.[21] The underlying contradictions revealed in my interview narratives actually challenge the idea that groups are either oppressed or privileged. That dichotomy is too simplistic. Instead, there are shades of oppression, from invisibility to marginalization, from anti-Zionism to overt anti-Semitism. All anti-Semitism is not created equal. American Jewish feminists often experience these complexities in the way social power and status operates.

These stories raise important questions about the complexities of social identities, group loyalties, and global communities. The women I interviewed felt conflicted between loyalties to Israel and to the feminist movement. They also disagreed on distinguishing between anti-Semitism and anti-Zionism. This confusion reflects their own ambivalences toward Israel and a sense of worldwide Jewish community. Being confronted with their own difference, as Jews within the women's movement, forces them to examine the meaning that being Jewish holds for them.

Also, given the murky and dynamic nature of memory, it is possible to look back on interactions in one's life as rooted in anti-Semitism without being sure of other people's motives. As this cohort became more sensitive to multicultural discourses, they seemed to develop an understanding of themselves as part of an "othered" people. In other words, being Jewish became an identity of subordination. The "matrix of oppression" discourse of their generation of feminists was eventually translated into their understanding of themselves as Jews.

It is no wonder that these Jewish second-wave feminists sometimes appear ambivalent about the role of Israel, feminism, and anti-Semitism in their political frameworks. "Jew" is not a clear-cut identity category, but rather some complex combination of ethnicity, culture, and religion. The Left has often denied that Jews are an othered group. Instead, Jews are considered just another religion among the white privileged masses. Academic women's studies examines hybrid identities and oppression with little attention to how Jewish women fit into these processes. Jewish women cannot easily find themselves represented in women's studies or the American and international women's movements. Some of the stories presented in earlier chapters show the struggle to find one's place as an insider within Jewish communities. In this chapter, however, my interviewees reveal a dance between being an insider and an outsider in feminist communities.

Chapter Four

PATRIARCHAL OPPOSERS

*Constructing Jewish
Feminist Masculinities*

Men can be feminists, too. Anyone who believes that women
should be equal partners with men in society—and is willing to act on
that belief—is a feminist, and that includes men. There were many male
activists who fought on behalf of women's rights in the 1970s.

I interviewed a small number of Jewish men who participated in this
struggle. The five men I will introduce below have devoted just as much
energy to fighting gender inequality as any feminist woman. In fact, all of
them have continued their activism until this day. There is a difference in
terminology, though. Many of the men I interviewed do not use the term
"feminist" to describe themselves. To distinguish themselves from feminists
who are women, they call themselves "profeminist" men.[1]

This chapter explores constructions of Jewish masculinity from the perspectives of profeminist Jewish men. These men all relate, in some way,
to the existence of a Jewish masculinity that is distinct from American or
mainstream masculinity. They articulate what I call a "discourse of Jewish
alternative masculinity." What are some specifics of this notion of Jewish
masculinity? Jewish men are seen as nonviolent, gentle, intellectual, and
sensitive, and thus different from the "usual" types of men that feminists
critique. When articulating this discourse (as with the discourse of Jewish-
feminist congruence discussed in chapter two), interviewees claim that

there are commonalities between being Jewish and being feminist that are specific to men.

It is important to note that I do not intend to make any generalizations about what Jewish men are like and who they are as a group. I am not personally claiming that these ideas about Jewish men are true. Cultural discourses are not hard-and-fast realities. In fact, I contend that the discourse of Jewish alternative masculinity simplifies the diversity of Jewish men and falsely depicts American Jewish masculinity as a monolith.

Do the men I interviewed truly believe in this vision of Jewish masculinity? Yes and no, as you will read in their words below. The interviewees in this chapter express varying degrees of belief and disbelief in the discourse of Jewish alternative masculinity; each respondent relates to it in his own way. One thing is true, though: as I will show, this discourse is readily found in literature about Jewish men.

LOOKING BACK AT THE PROFEMINIST MEN'S MOVEMENT

In the early 1970s, as the women's liberation movement was burgeoning, men banded together to engage in feminist politics.[2] Members of the early men's movement formed alliances with women feminists to protest male violence, sexual harassment, and workplace inequality, and to support the Equal Rights Amendment and abortion rights. Their methods were similar to those of the women's liberation movement. They formed consciousness-raising groups and grassroots organizations, and published newsletters, magazines, and books pertaining to gender inequality. The men I interviewed were involved in various aspects of this loosely formed men's movement: the anti–violence against women movement, the abortion rights movement, the battered women's shelter movement, and the pro–Equal Rights Amendment movement.

In the late 1970s, the men's movement split off into various factions, including the antifeminist men's rights movement and the mythopoetic men's movement.[3] Nevertheless, the anti-sexist/profeminist men's movement remained and is still going strong. In fact, the men in this chapter still belong to profeminist organizations.

TOWARD A THEORY OF JEWISH MASCULINITY

Whether they knew it or not, the men I interviewed were speaking within the genre of masculinity theory. Before getting to the interviews themselves, I think it is important to briefly lay out masculinity theory to help contextualize the interview narratives.

Whereas gender studies has explored power dynamics between women and men, the recent proliferation of literature on men and masculinity has been particularly focused on exploring hierarchies between men. The concept of hegemonic masculinity, first developed by Tim Carrigan, Bob Connell, and John Lee, is used to explain processes of stratification among groups of men.[4] Connell used this concept in *Gender and Power* to demonstrate that "the interplay between different forms of masculinity is an important part of how a patriarchal social order works."[5] Hegemonic masculinity is described as the construction of masculinity among elite members of society, delivering not only control of women but also control of other men. It is a "culturally exalted" form of masculinity, perceived in public and fantasy figures, which serves as a standard against which all men measure their masculine worth.[6]

The men with the most power in society achieve ascendancy over other groups of men through the creation of ideals of masculinity, embodied in the United States by cultural icons such as Arnold Schwarzenegger, James Dean, John Wayne, and Sylvester Stallone. Hegemonic masculinity comprises traits such as physical aggressiveness, toughness, competition, hostility to homosexuality, and sexual objectification of women.[7] It is about ways of being male that predominate in specific social settings. These perceived traits are given status as constituting authentic masculinity. Other forms of masculinity, referred to in the literature as subordinated masculinities, are perceived as somehow less manly. The men I interviewed present Jewish masculinity as a form of subordinated masculinity.

Both hegemonic and subordinated masculinities are culturally and temporally specific, defined differently in different social contexts. They are cultural discourses, not distinct and fixed personality types. In other words, subordinated masculinities—by class, ethnicity, race, or sexual orientation—should not be confused with subordinated men. To suggest the concept of Jewish alternative masculinity is not to say that most Jewish men themselves conform to it. The social construction of masculinity is not carried out only by mainstream men; marginalized men participate in its construction as well. Thus the relationship of nonhegemonic men to the concept of hegemonic masculinity is a significant aspect of the making of masculine identities.

This chapter looks at the identities of men who relate to masculine ideals as members of a historically subordinated group—Jews—but also as profeminists. In these two ways, they might be considered participants in the construction of subordinated masculinities. On the other hand, they are all white, middle-class, and heterosexual and thus fall into some hegemonic identity categories.

Ethnic/racial inequality goes hand in hand with gender oppression, through stereotypes or controlling images. Such images often portray the men and/or the women of marginalized groups in contradictory and limiting ways, especially in relation to gender and sexuality.[8] In contemporary times, Jewish men are frequently depicted with contradictory images. On the one hand, they have been portrayed as powerful, rich, and conspiring to take control of the world (from exaggerations about the "Jewish Hollywood elite" to *The Protocols of the Elders of Zion*). On the other hand, they are often portrayed as weak, effeminate, or neurotic (for example, Woody Allen characters and other film and TV depictions).

Partly because of societal images such as these, Jewish men have a complicated and historically changing relationship to masculinity.[9] They have endured a history of anti-Semitic imagery that has attacked their manhood. "If masculinity requires proof for white Anglo-Saxon Protestant men, then for Jewish men the problem was even more acute. Because Jewish men were understood by white Anglo-Saxon Protestant society to come from a religious culture that stressed morality and literacy, they were seen as emasculated, and such stereotyped presumptions led to stereotypes about Jewish men."[10] Anti-Semitic stereotypes in Europe associated Jewish men with women; from medieval times in Europe, it was also widely believed that Jewish men menstruated.[11] In some parts of early modern Europe, the little finger was referred to as "the Jew."[12] Jewish men's public image was caught between multiple controlling images. They were considered nonsexual, queer, or sexually predatory.

Where do all of these images leave Jewish men in relation to gender oppression? "We are often viewed as weak, not sexual; in fact, emasculated," says Robert Rosenberg. "Jewish women are often seen as strong, powerful, and in some mysterious way 'outside of sexism.' On the other hand, Jewish men are trained to be argumentative, rational thinkers, something which is in some sense very male. Yet we are often considered the most sensitive and least sexist of men. Some people might think Jewish men need feminism least of all, while others might think we need it the most. The truth, of course, lies somewhere in between."[13] There seems to be confusion about just what Jewish men are really about. The literature discussed so far does consider Jewish masculinity to be a unique and subordinated form of masculinity. However, there is no conclusion drawn about the content of that form.

Daniel Boyarin asserts that despite the anti-Semitic stereotype of Jewish men as unmanly, within Jewish culture masculine ideals were declared in opposition to gentile masculinity: "Premodern Jewish culture, I will argue, frequently represented ideal Jewish men as feminized through various discursive means. This is not, moreover, a representation that carries with it any hint of internalized contempt or self-hatred. Quite the opposite; it was through this mode of conscious alternative gendering that Jewish culture frequently asserted its identity over-against its surroundings."[14] The ideal Jewish man was a countertype to the European model of "activity, domination, and aggressiveness as 'manly' and gentleness and passivity as emasculate or effeminate."[15] Although this Jewish oppositional identity was "unmanning," it was not desexualizing. Boyarin traces this European Jewish inversion of hegemonic gender roles back to rabbinic texts.

Boyarin further argues that the early modern Eastern European Jewish paradigm "has something compelling to offer us in our current moment of search for a feminist reconstruction of male subjectivity."[16] It is not my aim to agree with him in stating that Jewish masculinity is more sympathetic to feminism, although my interviewees do discuss this idea from different vantage points. While Boyarin looks to the gender paradigms of rabbinic culture as "a resource in the radical reconstruction of male subjectivities that feminism calls for," he also acknowledges that this culture has been oppressive to women as well.[17]

JEWISH PROFEMINIST MEN TELL THEIR STORIES

When I asked Jewish profeminist men to talk about the relationship between their Jewish and feminist identities, they focused on what it means to be a Jewish man. There was some agreement with Boyarin's notion that paradigms of masculinity within Jewish culture are compatible with more feminist ideals of masculinity. At the same time, however, they deconstruct their own narratives of Jewish-feminist congruence and question the extent to which those ideas are grounded in reality. These men positioned themselves variously in relation to the discourse of Jewish alternative masculinity; their narratives include uncritical assertions, self-critical claims, and total disavowals of this discourse.

Daniel and Mark Theorize Jewish Alternative Masculinity

Daniel was raised in a suburban Conservative Jewish community. He claims that his Jewish identity has always "waxed and waned," although he had a religiously active Jewish upbringing. Daniel says about his Jewish identity, "I consider myself a very spiritually shallow person and live a very secular humanist life." Growing up, he felt a sense of shame that the Jews "allowed themselves to be killed" during the Holocaust, so he was extremely pleased to learn as an adult about the Jewish resistance fighters who fought back against the Nazi regime. He connects this shame to his gender; as a boy, he considered it particularly shameful to learn that Jews did not defend themselves physically.

For Daniel, the important components of being a Jewish man include ethics, politics, justice, and intellect. As a progressive academic, he shares all of these values. Daniel emphasizes an intellectual orientation in his description of Jewish men. He also draws on a discourse of post-Holocaust social justice that he feels impels Jews to participate in progressive politics: "I think being a Jewish man means not being a mainstream man . . . not falling under the category of hegemonic definition . . . I think the sort of bookishness, the learning stuff is one part. I thought the political ethical imperative of 'never again' was another part. And there's the kind of, we don't subscribe to the traditional anti-intellectualism, and we don't subscribe to the traditional me-first-ism. So those are components of a Jewish masculinity as an alternative to hegemonic masculinity . . . I think Judaism provides a foundation for an alternative vision of masculinity, a masculinity that can be ethical." Daniel mixes the past and the present here in portraying Jewish masculinity, beginning some sentences with "I think" and others with "I thought." This simultaneous avowal of and distancing from the discourse of Jewish alternative masculinity may reveal an underlying uncertainty in his own statements.

Daniel describes ways in which Jewishness is compatible with feminism. He alleges that even within a patriarchal context, Jewish communities have historically supported women. He proposes that Jewish women of his generation were raised with support for professional and educational aspirations. He surmises that these ambitions were stifled by sexist American society, thereby making feminism a useful outcome: "I think there were ways in which Judaism was a natural for feminism . . . Jewish women were much more encouraged, despite the patriarchy of the religion, much more encouraged to go to college . . . much more encouraged to be smart, to not hide it, to be careerist, and suddenly it's choked off by patriarchy. So there's ways in which there's thwarted ambition." Even though Daniel is referring here to the lives of women, he is actually making a statement about Jewish masculinity. He does so by implicitly claiming that Jewish men support the success of the women in their lives.

Daniel also acknowledges the historical reality of patriarchal Judaism. He refers to the ritual of circumcision and a traditional verse from the prayer book as reminders of the patriarchal history of Judaism. He distinguishes between Jewish men and "hegemonic men" but acknowledges that Jewish men possess power over women, specifically Jewish women: "Being a Jewish man, vis-à-vis Jewish women, [is] still quite a patriarchal relationship . . . So on the one hand, Jewish masculinity does have some possible foundations on which to build an alternative masculinity to the hegemonic version. Not to say it's always taken, but it's possible. On the other hand, there are components within Judaism, of course, that, like the circumcision, like the reproduction of patriarchy, that are about male domination and about women's inequality and subordination. And I don't have to remind people about the certain 'Thank God I'm not a woman' stuff."[18] Daniel's earlier articulation of the notion of coherence between Jewish masculinity and feminism refers to Jewish culture. Here, however, he critically assesses this notion in light of the reality of sexism within the Jewish religion.

Daniel contrasts the interplay between gender relations and gender equality in Jewish culture and American culture: "So it's funny because what I was saying before is that American culture has given women part A of feminism—equal opportunity—but not B, the transformation of gender relations that would include the transformation of masculinity. Judaism offers B without A, which is to say it gives men the basis on which to construct the new definition of masculinity, but it doesn't give women the equal opportunity [laughing] . . . So certainly, it's true that Jewish men can be real men vis-à-vis women. And be just as oppressive, just as patriarchal, and just as stubborn and impervious about it as hegemonic men. No question about that. An alternative sense of masculinity in the abstract doesn't necessarily play out as an alternative in gender relations." In other words, although the discourse of Jewish alternative masculinity provides a nonnormative masculine ideal, its subversive potential is weakened by the real-life subordination of Jewish women.

Mark, another man I interviewed, also describes a culture of Jewish masculinity that differs from mainstream American masculinity. Like Daniel, he invokes this discourse of Jewish alternative masculinity in linking his feminism to his Jewish cultural background. Both of Mark's parents are non-Orthodox children of Orthodox immigrants, and they raised him with conflicting views about Judaism. He was active in synagogue life as a child. He now belongs to a congregation in which he feels very comfortable because "there's a bunch of radicals there who are no more religious than I am."

Mark traces respect for women back to early Jewish history, interpreting a protofeminist paradigm in ancient rabbinic culture. He credits the authors of the Jewish rabbinic texts with being inclined to listen to women: "I actually think there's strong roots of feminism in Judaism . . . There are many stories about this, like the rabbi's daughter, I think, he wrote her into the canon, into his rabbinic writings.[19] And now it's been discovered that she was actually a famous rabbinical person . . . If a woman got up and argued with a rabbi, and the argument made sense, in my idealization, that rabbi would say, 'Oh, that makes sense.' There's something in the Jewish tradition about that . . . But there's a respect for the woman who says something. Well, that's part of feminism . . . Women spoke up and men listened. Jewish men, I think, were more likely to listen just like the rabbi was more likely to listen to his daughter or somebody." Like Daniel, Mark echoes the theme of Jewish men's respect for women's intellect and capability.

Mark then returns to contemporary times to claim a Jewish foundation for being a profeminist man: "Men who are supporting gender equity are speaking up against domination, but not from a position of being oppressed. So what men are saying is, 'This is right. We will listen to what the oppressed group is saying, and then we will think about the way that we're dominating because we're basically opposed to domination. If they're telling us that we're dominating in this way, then we need to listen and do something about that.' Now, that's a Jewish—there are Jewish roots to that attitude, that kind of openness."

Mark makes a connection between Jewishness and progressive politics by linking, more explicitly than Daniel, norms for Jewish men with feminist and radical ideologies. In the following excerpt, he enunciates an antiviolent dimension of the Jewish masculinity discourse. Notice, however, that he distinguishes between his perception of Jewish men and the reality that some Jewish men are physically abusive: "Whatever it is that Jewish men are supposed to do has some parallels with feminism. So I would find it extremely weird that a Jewish man were beating his wife . . . Now I know that Jewish men beat their wives, but it's still not my sense of what goes into being a Jewish man. So I think that just like there's a set of overlapping things with radical politics, I think there's a set of things with feminism that makes a lot of sense in the Jewish tradition." Here Mark juxtaposes thinking that Jewishness overlaps with feminism with knowing that it is not always true. While he submits that Jewish men do not beat their wives, he also problematizes that claim, both embracing the discourse of Jewish alternative masculinity and questioning it.

Mark asserts that there are feminist elements to Jewish cultural norms for men by emphasizing the Jewish man's role in the family as a nonviolent father and husband. But as soon as he discloses his views on what a Jewish man should be, he qualifies them by calling them idealizations: "A lot of this is idealization. Because if you look at Jewish families across the country, I don't think you'd get a pure left-leaning feminist happy family. There are a lot of Jewish homeless youth out there who come from families where they were beaten. So I think a lot of it is idealization on my part." Implicit in this passage is Mark's indirect admission of his own middle-class perspective. He deconstructs the discourse of Jewish alternative masculinity that he has just enunciated by revealing the class bias of many of its assumptions.

Mark's narrative reveals the ambivalent nature of the discourse of Jewish alternative masculinity. He diminishes the accuracy of this discourse by naming it a fantasy. Furthermore, Mark told me that he feels he has created "out of his dreams" a romanticized history of Judaism that focuses on liberation; this contradicts his portrayal of Judaism as integrally linked to feminism and radicalism. Mark gave me the impression that he came to realize his ambivalence during the course of our conversation.

Mark and Daniel confined their discussion to Jewish men in general. It is not clear that they see themselves, personally, as different from non-Jewish men. Their depictions of Jewish men remain at the theoretical level and do not appear to be internalized into their own gender identities. However, although their narratives are not self-directed, they are nonetheless discursive expressions of Mark's and Daniel's identities as members of the social group they describe. These narratives reflect on contemporary American ideas about masculinity and perceptions of the place of subgroups, such as Jews, within that. As such, they are articulations of Jewish cultural models of masculinity.

Sam, the Jewish Boy Outsider

In contrast to Daniel and Mark, Sam's narratives about Jewish masculinity are more personalized and related to his own life experiences. Sam is the son of immigrant parents who lived through the Holocaust. Being the child of Holocaust survivors is his "core identity," and he feels that it is inseparable from his Jewish identity. His mother's and father's religious background and outlook were very different; one was from an assimilated German family, and the other from a Polish Orthodox *shtetl* (Eastern European Jewish village). In recalling his Jewish upbringing, Sam said, "My Jewish identity is very much cultural, historical, Holocaust survivor." Sam now belongs to a synagogue and has been providing his children with a Jewish education.

Sam also evokes the discourse of Jewish alternative masculinity, but unlike Daniel and Mark, he uses as his reference point his own experience of alienation from American gender norms. Sam recalls feeling like an outsider as he was growing up, which he partially attributes to being Jewish. Because he felt he was different from other males, the feminist critique of masculinity compelled him: "I mean, there were a lot of men being disturbed, scared, however you want to put it, by women's liberation. But some of us thought there might be something more positive. And a lot of that had to do with my Jewish identity, because the feminist critique of mainstream models of masculinity was something I was happy to join in critiquing. Because it sure wasn't me. It was an image of masculinity that also was a very WASP model and oppressive to Jews as well . . . So then finding other men and women who were criticizing that, more receptive to the kind of person I was, it was finding a home more than anything else." Here he is recalling the development of his own individual gender identity and making sense of it within a social framework. As someone who felt like a misfit, he found that feminism allowed him to feel secure in his own identity by critiquing masculinity.

Sam's narrative suggests an embodied subject in conflict with non-Jewish culture. Sam sees the Jewish man as living in tension with American culture. The subject of anti-Semitism forms the subtext of his musings about Jewish masculinity: "From the perspective of non-Jewish culture, a Jewish male identity is a feminized identity. It's the scholar, the weakling, the intellectual . . . The Jewish man struggles under the sort of mainstream culture's stigma of effeminacy, always that inferiority. He's not a real man under mainstream culture's terms . . . But it's a catch-22, double-bind situation. 'Cause the Jewish man is the scholar, the intellectual and all that, and that's not the mainstream culture's image of masculinity. So if you're making it on your culture's terms, you're not making it on the mainstream culture's terms." Although Sam says that the Jewish man is feminized by the outside culture, he himself proudly constructs Jewish masculinity in opposition to that culture. Here he seems to affirm the reality of Jewish alternative masculinity.

Sam then goes on to delineate how his thinking about Jewish masculinity has developed over time and become more critical. Although he once thought that Jewish men were more compatible with a feminist model of masculinity, he has come to question the particulars of that idea. He still proposes that there is a Jewish model of masculinity, but not that it is more feminist: "So it took me a long, long time to finally get that some of the critique [of mainstream masculinity] also applied to me and to the Jewish community. The specific lyrics might be different, but there were real commonalities, too, in terms of patriarchal culture . . . So yeah, it became clear to me that we Jewish men weren't rowdy and physically competitive and boisterous and physically violent, but I later learned that there is violence in the Jewish community as well. But we certainly engaged in sort of intellectual and can-you-top-this in terms of telling the best joke or the best story rather than shooting hoops in front of them. So that gradually penetrated into my consciousness . . . It took me a while to realize the trap of that easy identification, 'cause I wasn't dealing with specifically Jewish aspects of patriarchal consciousness and behavior, which are all too present." The flipside to the purported intellectual orientation of Jewish men is intellectual domination. Jewish men are still "real men," as Sam says, not immune to the privileges of male power. Although Sam critiques some aspects of the discourse of Jewish alternative masculinity, he does not reject it completely.

Steven Deconstructs Alternative Jewish Masculinity

Like all of the men in this chapter, Steven grew up in a highly Jewish environment, in terms of his social networks and neighborhood. In describing his Jewish background, Steven said, "I'm definitely more explicitly Jewish than my parents, and I think more spiritually based in my Judaism." He describes his childhood relationship to Jewishness with complexity: "Although there was kind of a strong bent toward assimilation, it was also within a very Jewish context . . . So it wasn't strongly religious, but culturally it was very strongly Jewish."

While the three tellers discussed so far—Daniel, Mark, and Sam—voice some ambivalence about the discourse of Jewish alternative masculinity, their identification with it is unquestionable. Steven, on the other hand, completely removes himself from this discourse, deconstructing it without claiming any of it as based in truth. He refutes what the others say about

Jewish men, maintaining that the characteristics they cite are not particular to Jewish men but apply to the middle class in general.

During the interview, when I commented to Steven that he was unlike the other informants in that he did not seem to view Jewish men as possessing difference, he responded: "And I think that's partly because I see the core of masculinity being control. And some men are told that they should do it physically, and some men are told they should do it verbally, and others are told they should do it financially or intellectually. But understanding the dynamics of violence, of violence in relationships especially, that it doesn't really make much difference to the person being controlled, what tools you're using. And so I'm not about to make a big difference between verbally and emotionally and intellectually abusing somebody and physically abusing them. And I think Jewish men are taught to be in control. Just as every, all the other men in this society are." Steven continued to explain that the image of Jewish men as less violent is a "stereotype" that allows the Jewish community to remain in denial about domestic violence. If Jewish men are not physically aggressive, he asks, then how can there be domestic violence in the Jewish community? In contrast to Sam, he recalls that he fit into the dominant models of masculinity "too well" when he was growing up, and that he has worked hard to unlearn that as a profeminist adult.

Steven applies his feminist lens to Jewishness in a much more critical way than the others. According to him, not only are Jewish men no different from hegemonic men, but feminism and Jewishness are also incompatible: "The Judaism that I bring to feminism is more general in terms of social justice and things like that; whereas the feminism I bring to Judaism is much more specific and detailed . . . I think as a Jewish community over the last thirty years, we've had to modify Judaism in light of our feminist understanding. But we haven't had to modify feminism very much in light of our Jewish understanding. Because Judaism doesn't have a history of equality, of gender justice." Steven presents a different view here of Jewish history than other interviewees who claimed a feminist countertradition in Jewish religious and cultural history.

In the previous excerpt, Steven denies that there is a history of equality in Judaism, whereas in the next excerpt he presents a bleak view of the impact of feminism on the Jewish community today: "Everything I learned growing up about Judaism had men in control, and men naturally at the top of the hierarchy. So I didn't have any roots in Judaism that would lead me to feminism. And I've yet to meet anybody who has . . . There doesn't seem to be a core of feminism deep within Judaism any place that I can see . . . I mean, obviously there's lots of Jews who are feminists, but they're not influencing the institutional structures of the community. Or not in any significant way." Unlike Daniel, Mark, and Sam, Steven does not communicate ambivalently. He is unique in his total rejection of the concepts of Jewish alternative masculinity and Jewish-feminist congruence. He presented an unambiguously critical view of Judaism and seemed frustrated at what he perceives as resistance in the Jewish community to examining issues of gender.

Gerald: Feminist, or Not?

The final interviewee to be discussed, Gerald, was the first to portray Jewish men according to negative stereotypes. Although he calls himself a feminist, many of his viewpoints might make the reader question this identification. Gerald grew up in a working-class Jewish neighborhood, the son of poor immigrant parents. He says that his parents were "assimilationists" who "never stepped foot inside a synagogue except for [his] bar-mitzvah day." He enrolled himself in Hebrew school to prepare for his bar-mitzvah despite his parents' protests that they could not afford it. He exhibited negative feelings toward Jews, stemming from his unhappy childhood: "The problem was poverty was a greater influence on me than Judaism."

He was a young child during the Holocaust and remembers hearing about relatives being "put in ovens" and other horrible reports about friends and family in Europe. The terror of the Holocaust has left an indelible mark on him: "I had an existential angst about being Jewish. I thought that I could be killed at any time. My dreams at night, the Nazis were on the fire escape talking about how to get in the apartment to get me and my family." The Holocaust also impelled Gerald to become an activist. He links his feminism to Jewishness through the common thread of otherness: "There but for the grace of God, said I, would have gone I, were I living in Nazi Germany, Poland, any of Eastern Europe, etcetera. So I'm committed to stopping crazy lethal hatred of people. When I read feminist literature, I saw that women suffered a form of discrimination and exclusion from opportunities the likes of which I had earlier easily identified as oppressing people of color. And Jews." Here Gerald articulates the typical claim that being a member of a subordinated group, in this case Jews, influences a person's tendency toward activism.

Gerald stands out from the other men in that he presents a negative image of Jewish masculinity. Because he switched between past and present tense, it was unclear whether he was describing formerly held views or if he still believed his depiction of Jewish men. While Daniel, Mark, and Sam portray Jewish men in a positive light, and Steven insists that they are not unlike non-Jewish men, Gerald has nothing positive to say about Jewish masculinity. He seems to have internalized negative stereotypes.

Gerald depicts hegemonic masculinity in opposition to Jewish masculinity, which was typical in the interview narratives. What is unusual in his case is that he seems to be speaking from a position of hegemonic masculinity and accepting the stereotypical construction of Jewish masculinity: "Like most men, I'm very protective of my mother. Very protective of my wife. If I had a daughter, my daughter. Women in general. The male role is to protect women. So there was a male role as opposed to Jewishness. Jewish men, I don't think, as a matter of fact, I didn't like Jewish men's behavior towards women. I thought it was pathetic and not very sexy. I thought Jewish men lost out . . . They weren't sexy. They weren't powerful . . . Who were the Jewish men who attracted women? John Garfield, in boxing. All the men who were attractive were gangsters and tough men." Gerald concurs with the discourse of Jewish masculinity by characterizing Jewish men as nonaggressive. He sees them as somehow less masculine than other men, outside the typical masculine norms. But for him, this is a source of shame, since Jewish men supposedly do not conform to the traditional gender roles that he defines in the previous passage.

This chapter looks at Jewish profeminist men "talking masculinity." What I have called the "discourse of Jewish alternative masculinity" is a kind of discourse of Jewish-feminist congruence (see chapter two) because it claims that feminism and Jewish masculine culture are complementary.

Jewish feminist men occupy a unique position in relation to both feminism and Jewishness. They are simultaneously in power and disempowered. As Jews, they are minority men. Yet they also acknowledge their power in relation to Jewish women. Their approach to understanding the intersections of Jewish and feminist identities is different from the approaches of the women explored in previous chapters, because they emphasize the meanings of their gender identities.

What are the elements of this discourse of Jewish alternative masculinity that they articulate? A primary distinction drawn between Jewish and non-Jewish men involves physicality, aggression, and violence. Jewish men are seen as less athletic, less violent, and less aggressive overall. The association of masculinity with violence seems particularly prevalent in the interview narratives, perhaps because a focus of the profeminist men's movement has been on eradicating violence against women.

A justification used to explain the perceived lack of physicality among Jewish men is that Jewish tradition values intellect over physical virility. The men I interviewed support this claim with references to Jewish "bookishness" and intellectualism. Another claim made is that Jewish men are taught ethics, through a Judaic value of social justice in general, and through feminism more specifically. This connection allows Jewish profeminist men to overcome the gap between their maleness and their feminist activism by claiming that feminism and Jewish masculine culture are naturally complementary. However, they do not question how "alternative" Jewish men really are when it comes to the main marker of middle-class masculinity in our society—economic success.

It is not important for my analysis to evaluate whether there is a reality behind the discourse of Jewish alternative masculinity. The men themselves construct this discourse ambivalently. While the men I interviewed collectively describe a notion of Jewish masculinity as alternative to the hegemonic model, none of them make these statements uncritically and without reservation. They draw from a cultural discourse of Jewish masculinity and have a vested interest in that discourse because it supports their identity as male feminists. Yet they ultimately reveal the knowledge that they are repeating generalizations and stereotypes. Thus the discourse of Jewish alternative masculinity, as it is proposed in the interview narratives, is simultaneously deconstructed and disavowed.

All of these constructions of Jewish masculinity are in reaction to the views of the majority culture and historical discourses. Identities are formed in ambivalent ways, not in a vacuum, but in reaction to cultural discourses created from within and outside one's group. My interviewees' ambivalence about how Jews, and they themselves, fit into this framework serves to underscore the dynamic, multifaceted, and historically and culturally produced nature of discourses of gender. This discourse is obviously a site of complex feelings for the men in this chapter; as a narrative of identity, it is indicative of the contradictions and complexities of the self.

Conclusion

What people say about themselves defines them. This book is based on people talking about themselves, but it is only a snapshot in time. It is not a complete picture of self-definition. Instead, it is about a cohort of people and the social construction of their identities. You have just read about how people make sense of being both Jews and feminist activists. You now know that there are many ways in which Jewish feminists interpret the meanings of these two identities.

I discovered a variety of approaches to Judaism and feminism among the thirty participants in this study. Some informants demonstrated an ongoing struggle to reconcile the conflicts between Judaism and feminism, focusing their feminist activism in the synagogue and Jewish organizations. Others found inspiration for their activism in Judaism or their Jewish upbringing.

Another important theme of this book is the search for a comfortable niche among both activist and Jewish communities. Jews have been significant to the shaping of the American feminist movement. Yet their importance, as Jews, has not been sufficiently recognized. Jewish women still experience marginalization within feminist communities.

Also, the definitions of what it means to be Jewish are manifold. Just among the feminists presented in this book, there are changing definitions of being a Jew. Some are so secular and assimilated that they claim reading about the Holocaust is the only "Jewish thing" they do. Others define themselves as religious and practice Jewish rituals. Among ethnic groups and religious groups, Jews are a special case, an odd combination of religion and ethnicity. But as the people in this group make clear, Jewishness does not fit neatly into either category.

The life history interview method uncovers accounts of the changeable nature of identities. Each informant describes a past with shifting Jewish and feminist identities. At least on the surface, however, their Jewish identities seem to have fluctuated more than their feminist identities throughout their lives. They recalled waxing and waning religiosity and connections to Jewishness. Jewish identity must be understood as one aspect of a multifaceted, changing, and complex self.

Their Jewish identities have formed partially in response to shifting cultural representations of Jewish difference in America. The changes within American Judaism that have taken place throughout the informants' lifetimes have also affected their sense of Jewishness. Since my sample of informants spans a wide age range, these changes have affected them differently.

The construction of identities is an ongoing navigation of multiple cultural discourses. The process of reinterpreting and integrating various discourses of identities results in complex perspectives on the relationship between Jewishness and feminism.

Although I set out to examine whether Jewish feminists find these two facets of themselves to be in discord or in harmony, the picture turned out to be much more complicated. I found that the same individuals may claim that Jewishness and feminism are both congruent and dissonant, or that they have changed their position on this at various points in their lives. The divergence of approaches and understandings of this relationship among my respondents points to the multiple meanings and configurations of interlocking identities.

What I have captured in this work is not so much the informants' actual identities, but rather a glimpse of the presentation of their identities. My analysis is based on spoken narratives and thus is restricted to the medium of language as an expression of identity. The spoken word offers an incomplete, more fixed and neat version of human subjectivity. However, I am unable to read the informants' minds, and thus I am reliant on interview data as a window into their subjectivity.

This study is therefore actually about narratives of identity. The relationship between Jewish and feminist identities emerges here through the vocalization of shared cultural discourses. Although I have presented these discourses in the context of the informants' individual life stories, I do not mean to equate individuals with discourses. Individuals can and do voice multiple discourses. And culture is created by groups, not individuals.

The findings of this study cannot be separated from the historical moment in which it occurred and the events that have shaped the informants' lives. The era has passed in which the liberation of women is seen as antithetical to Jewish concerns. The feminist transformation of Judaism, under way now for more than forty years, has been an influence on the Jewish identities of all of the informants, regardless of their Jewish affiliations. The rise of the discourse of multiculturalism and increased awareness of ethnic identities has also been an influence on their understandings of themselves as American Jews.

Little research exists on either Jewish feminist identities or the relationship between gender and Jewish identity. Despite a history of gender inequality within Judaism, this study demonstrates that Jewish feminists can find coherence in these identities. Jewishness means different things to different people, and it can be integrated with other identities, including variously defined feminist identities.

The life histories examined in this work attest to the impact of experiences with Jewish institutions on one's Jewish identity. Negative and positive interactions with rabbis and other Jewish leaders have the effect of either drawing people closer to Judaism and the Jewish institutional world or pushing them away from it. Gender matters; the way girls and women were treated and portrayed in the Jewish world left its mark on their conceptions of Jewishness.

Jews have been largely left out of the conversation about intersectionality in women's studies. This conversation has emphasized the interaction between gender, class, and race, yet it has not examined the role of religious identities. Although the women I interviewed are white and middle-class, they are not Christian; their Jewishness places them outside the mainstream American unmarked category and makes them a minority. They have complex relationships to hegemonic American definitions of race, religion, and ethnicity. Their ambivalence about how to place themselves among these categories of identity comes through in the interview accounts.

By participating in interviews about gender, feminism, and Jewishness, the participants in this study have contributed to the discussion among feminists about the relationship between gender and other identities. They have demonstrated how their experiences as Jews influence their experiences as women and men. Just as gender matters for understanding Jewish identity, Jewishness matters for understanding gender. Their narratives show that being Jewish provides a particular cultural background and a particular lens on being female and male.

This creative interweaving of identities applies to how Jewish feminists relate Jewishness to feminism. They must make sense of contested identities and disparate affiliations, and they use a variety of strategies to negotiate this challenge. In so doing, they participate in the continued formation of cultural discourses of identity. Like all of us, the people who share their stories in this book are continually forging their identities. Like all of us, they are creating culture every day.

Appendix: Biographical Sketches

Alice

Alice is a social worker in the nonprofit sector. She was an activist in the antiwar movement and the civil rights movement. When she realized the extent of the sexism in those movements, she turned to feminism. She became active in the early battered women's movement, helping to create battered women's shelters in various cities. She then raised three children as a single mother, which required her to work full-time and give up much of her feminist volunteer work. Alice was raised by immigrant parents whose adherence to traditional gender roles she attributed to Judaism, although it may have been related more to their immigrant backgrounds. She describes her family upbringing as "High Holiday religious" because they went to services on holidays and kept kosher "up to a point," but "religion was never major in the household." As an adult, Alice describes herself as "a-religious" and expressed strong hostility toward her brother's Orthodox Jewish practices.

Ann

Ann was raised in a communist household; she is one of a number of "red diaper babies" in my sample.[1] She still identifies as a socialist and radical. On the other hand, she told me that her Jewish identity is "not that important." She is an academic who followed a somewhat typical activist path, participating in the antiwar movement, the civil rights movement, and then radical feminism. She is one of the few people in my sample who have remained with the same partner since before becoming an activist. She married her husband (another activist, now a union organizer) immediately after graduating college and is still with him today. They have two grown children.

Ann grew up in New York City, where, she said, "my Jewish education, my Jewish experience is minimal if not zilch." She described her Jewish upbringing: "It was sort of cultural—what foods you ate . . . most of [my parents'] friends were Jewish, or many of them were. And the conversation had that Jewish bent. But it was all on the level of culture, certainly not religion. You know my father was very antireligious [as part of his communist politics] . . . So I didn't have much of a Jewish identity."

Barbara

Barbara is one of only eight childless feminists I interviewed: "I made that decision early, never regretted it, and consider it the most significant event in my life that I was able to make that decision early and stick with it." Barbara did not want to be tied down by children and attributes the productivity and creativity she has enjoyed to being childless. She identifies as heterosexual and lives with her male partner.

Barbara is a freelance journalist of sorts, and an independent scholar. She considers herself a "scholar activist." She became involved in the civil rights movement while working on some educational projects in South Carolina in 1964. She was also an antiwar activist before her experiences in those movements led her to feminism: "Guys ten or twelve years younger were making decisions, we were typing . . . and I didn't know what I was going to do about this click experience."[2] Barbara's early feminist activism was related to education, advocating affirmative action and helping to set policies. She contributed to the founding of the field of women's studies at the university level. She was hired by organizations such as NOW and *Ms. Magazine*.[3]

When I asked Barbara to tell me her Jewish autobiography, she focused on her experiences with Jewish men. She said she had found in her life that Jewish men were not supportive of feminism. She generalized with some hostility about Jews and Jewish men. She insisted that in order to do justice to my topic, I should interview Jewish men from that era who are not feminist to find out their views. She was the only woman I interviewed who expressed such a view. In fact, she became very interested in this idea of Jewish men's hostility to feminism and continued to discuss it after the interview was over.

Brenda

Brenda, an academic, came out of the closet while a member of the Redstockings radical feminist group.[4] She was active in radical feminist politics in New York City before joining the gay liberation movement. She was then instrumental in protesting the heterosexism in the women's liberation movement. She came to identify herself as a radical lesbian feminist. While Brenda's interview is not directly quoted anywhere in this book, her interview informed my analysis.

Daniel

By the time Daniel was in high school, he was already an activist. His mother baked cookies for the after-school meetings of SDS (Students for a Democratic Society) that were held at his house.[5] But his turn to feminism came by an unexpected route. In the mid-1970s, at the beginning of the anti–violence against women movement, Daniel's girlfriend was a volunteer for a battered women's shelter. Daniel happened to own a van with a stick shift, and his girlfriend did not know how to drive it. So Daniel would frequently drive the van, in the middle of the night, to escort abused women from their homes to the hospital. This experience was a crucial turning point for him.

From that point on, Daniel decided to devote his energy to feminism. He worked with a group of men fighting violence against women before he moved into academia: "But the political impulse never wavered from that moment on. That was my struggle. That was the place I was gonna put my energy." He eventually became one of the founders of the field of men's studies and was active in a national organization of men fighting for gender equality. Like other profeminist men, Daniel has focused his activism on men's involvement in sexism: he has been involved in rape prevention and the battered women's movement and writes about homophobia and men's relations to each other.

Edith

Edith is a social worker whose volunteer work has enabled her to put her beliefs and values into action. She was a more reformist or liberal activist than many of the other people I interviewed, who tended toward the more radical style of activism. She attributes this to her status as an upper-middle-class mother and wife in the 1960s and regrets that she lacked the freedom and courage to pursue the more radical activism of the era. Edith was a member of NOW in the 1960s, and remembers participating in actions such as the march on Fifth Avenue in New York City.[6] She defines her passion as working to give voice to the voiceless. She took part in the civil rights and integration movements and also did "antipoverty work." After divorcing her husband decades ago, she came out as a lesbian and "radically redefined" who she was. Much of her more recent activism has centered around gay and lesbian rights, but also family-work issues and peace. "I grew up in a community that was very anti-Semitic, which made me very conscious of my Jewishness. I went to a college that wasn't anti-Semitic, but it was very Christian, which also made me conscious of my Jewishness. But it really has been only in the last eight years or so, maybe ten, that I have been very actively and progressively growing Jewish. And that my feminism and my Judaism have definitely come hand in hand." Edith is now active in a gay and lesbian synagogue and Jewish feminist organization. She is a practicing Jew whose volunteer life and social networks are concentrated around Jewish institutions.

Eleanor

Eleanor works in the nonprofit sector, a natural outgrowth of her activist interests in working with the poor. She is married to a man and is a mother and grandmother. Like many others, she was an activist in the anti–Vietnam War movement but left because of the sexism and betrayal she experienced: "In the antiwar movement, the women were baking cookies and the men were plotting strategy." When she was younger, Eleanor was a sociology professor; she taught some of the early classes on women and gender. She later left academia. In the 1970s, Eleanor identified as a socialist feminist and was involved with the initial conceptualization of sexual harassment as a social problem along with domestic violence activism.

Eleanor considers herself to be a secular Jew today. She was raised in a family with multiple Jewish orientations: secular grandparents and kosher parents who attended a Conservative synagogue and celebrated Jewish holidays, yet also had Christmas trees and exchanged Christmas presents. Eleanor experienced a lot of anti-Semitism growing up and described her father as "pretty anti-Israel from the very strange perspective that if you put so many Jews in one place it would be easier to kill them!"

Evelyn

Evelyn was one of the older activists I interviewed: she began her activist career in the 1940s. She was also one of the few who had been part of the Old Left as well as the New Left. Evelyn seemed somewhat resistant to the interview, repeatedly insisting that her feminism was not her most important political identification and that she was an activist for many causes. "My coming-of-age politically was during World War II . . . At each stage I moved into the Left politics of the moment . . . Feminism was just another political movement . . . Feminism is part of a whole series of political issues to which I attend and which need my attention. And while I have been a committed feminist, I often differ with positions that my friends take." Evelyn was part of a feminist collective on a university campus that provided her with lifelong friends.

Evelyn often felt out of step with other feminists because of her age. She has a daughter who was part of the second-wave feminist generation. She said, for example, that when there is a conflict between feminism and civil rights in connection with an issue, she is likely to side with civil rights. Nevertheless, she said that she is "totally committed to what I see as basic feminist theory and a feminist perspective on the world."

Gail

Gail, an academic whose research focuses on Jewish studies and women's studies, grew up attending a progressive Reconstructionist synagogue and was unaware of the sexism in Judaism: "And it was amazing, because when I was growing up, girls and boys had exactly the same training for bar- and bat-mitzvah. There was no difference. There was a woman who was president of the congregation when I was about bat-mitzvah age. There were boys and girls who were treated exactly the same in religious school, in the same classes. So it kind of came as a jolt to me that Judaism was as sexist as it is."

She described herself as a "hippie, radical, and antiwar activist" in the late 1960s. She later founded a women's center along with some other women from her consciousness-raising group and worked there as the director for many years. Gail traces her feminist consciousness back to her Orthodox grandmother, who told her: "You have to have your own money. And you have to always kind of have a sense of yourself and be in charge of yourself and don't let other people lead you around."

Gerald

Gerald, a former academic, works as a consultant on issues of diversity in hiring. Gerald expressed some resentment, even hostility, toward feminist women. Having been raised poor, he was happy to say that he is comfortably middle-class for the first time in his life. He identifies as heterosexual, lives with his female partner, and is a father. Like many of the other interviewees, Gerald was an antiwar and civil rights activist. He later organized profeminist men on behalf of the ERA and child-care reform. "So part of my work as a lefty, as a political countercultural revolutionary, as I thought of myself then, was to bring feminism to the political Left."

Janet

Janet is another interviewee who works with books, but as a librarian. When she was growing up in the 1950s, she was chosen to be the first girl to become bat-mitzvah in her synagogue; she was skilled at Hebrew, so they thought she would be a good example to quiet those who were opposed to b'not-mitzvah. Her en-trée into feminism was through her interest in theater and media, and through developing cable access programs, some on topics such as legalizing abortion and welfare rights. She filmed many feminist actions. She did not identify as a radical feminist, but considered herself an "equal pay for equal work feminist," as she put it. Janet explained why she did not engage in the radical politics of the time despite identifying with many of the causes: "At a certain point I did not engage myself in what was going on because there were so many conflicts. I did not always want to be in the middle of the conflicts." Janet was a member of the liberal feminist organization NOW.

Janet traces some of her political inclinations to the radical Jewish camp she attended as a child. She laughed at the thought that her parents probably had no idea of the camp's political bent, but sent her there because it was a Jewish camp. As an adult, Janet became involved in Jewish feminist groups within Jewish organizations. She began attending daily morning services after her brother died, and she developed a strong attachment to the synagogue community. From there, she became very involved in synagogue life, often serving in leadership positions: "And there was a point at which I said to myself, if anybody had told me ten years ago that I would be leading a morning *minyan* service in a Conservative synagogue, I would have told them they were nuts. And yet, it was the most natural thing in the world for me to be doing by that time."

Jennifer

Jennifer is a magnificent storyteller who helped organize my interviews with other women in her locale. She also fussed over me a great deal, playing the role of "Jewish mother" when I was sick with the flu. Jennifer is a retired academic who is chronically ill. Although she is not a religious Jew, she described her secular Jewish identity as a prominent, salient aspect of her life. Coincidentally, another woman I interviewed happened to mention Jennifer as an example of a "very Jewish" person against whom to contrast her own submerged Jewish identity. I took this to mean that Jennifer wears her Jewishness on her sleeve. This does not surprise me, as she is a very demonstrative person who is up-front about who she is.

Jennifer has an interesting take on her activist philosophy: she sees love as the central touchstone. She views her participation in the civil rights movement through that lens and has been an activist on behalf of gay and lesbian rights even though she is heterosexual. Jennifer was active in the founding of women's studies and also in consciousness-raising groups. An important part of her narrative was her multiple experiences as a victim of rape at different stages in her life. She grew up in a heavily Jewish neighborhood and milieu, and acknowledged that she was raped by Jewish men because those were the men in her social networks. Yet she also shared that she would not marry a Jewish man because of those experiences, even though she consciously knows that Jewish men are no more likely to be rapists than other men.

Jill

Jill works in the nonprofit sector, helping low-income people. Back in the 1970s, she was a radical lesbian feminist and was active in the founding of the women's theater movement. She was also active in the civil rights movement before joining the women's movement. Jill's initiation into the feminist movement was at a Redstockings speak-out about abortion in a West Village church basement in New York City in the 1960s. From there, she joined WITCH and became somewhat of a separatist.[7] However, she increasingly found herself out of step with that community in terms of her viewpoints. She was part of a thriving activist community in Greenwich Village. Yet once she fell in love with a man, she was dropped by her entire circle of feminist friends. Jill was hesitant to participate in my research until she spent a day with me because of the pain she had endured as a result of this experience.

"So around 1972 is when I really started to embrace my Judaism, or that I was Jewish. Not that I went to temple or anything, but I started to really identify myself as a Jewish radicalesbian feminist [laugh]. It's a mouthful!" Jill grew up in what she considered a very Jewish environment because of her neighborhood and social networks, but she felt like an outsider because her family was secular and unaffiliated while her friends were going to Hebrew school and becoming bar-mitzvah. Also, her parents were somewhat closeted leftists; as she put it, they were "a little pink." Jill is happy to have joined a humanistic Jewish organization, where she is quite involved.

Kathie

In the 1970s, Kathie was a multitalented activist. She was an activist-musician, performing music with politically radical messages for women audiences with her lesbian partner. She saw her feminism as part of a broader vision of social justice: "You know, my feminism was very connected to my socialism, to my lesbianism, communism. I mean, we used all those words. Because it was really a part of a vision of social change that encompassed everybody." Kathie belonged to a political research collective in the 1970s, where she lived with men and women who devoted their days to researching and publicizing various political issues, including gender issues.

Her activism has continued to be very eclectic. In the 1980s, Kathie saw herself as a "culture worker" organizing on behalf of women through a national women's music network. She spent time in different countries as a peace activist, picking coffee in Nicaragua for the Sandinistas and visiting Palestinian refugee camps. She belonged to Marxist study groups and the anti–nuclear power movement.[8] She continues to tie feminism to socialism and sees both as about "creating a world that is better for everybody." Still refusing to be labeled as one type of feminist activist, Kathie told me: "Yeah, my feminism is not just about women, and it's not just about one or two issues. It has that class analysis and a race analysis in it. My feminism is about liberation."

Lisa

Lisa, one of the older interviewees, was in her seventies at the time of the interview. Like a few of the others, she grew up in a Jewish communist community. Before becoming a feminist activist, she was a peace activist. Her entrée into feminism was through a Marxist feminist group and women's studies. She studied women's history and also organized for reproductive rights. Lisa told me that she was never a liberal feminist because she was interested in more fundamental changes in the family. In fact, she was disappointed that feminism had not been successful in completely changing the family.

Lisa was brought up in a secular Yiddishist community. She rebelled against the dogmatism of her family and their community. She saw being Jewish and being an ideologue as one and the same, and refused to send her children to *shula* or Yiddishist/socialist camps like those she had attended. She is a grandmother now and is married to her second husband. "Red diaper" Jewish families like hers were often adamantly secular, while stressing Jewish particularity at the same time: "I had to go to school on the Jewish holidays because they were so avidly antireligion. My father saw the Jews' religion as holding the working class back and antirevolutionary." Yet her parents spoke only Yiddish at home, so that she could learn it, and their social networks were entirely Jewish. This way of life stressed the Yiddish language and Ashkenazi Jewish culture, Jewish literature, and Jewish working-class organizations such as unions. Although Lisa critiqued the "fanaticism" of her father's beliefs, she clearly adopted many of the tenets of her socialist upbringing.

Mark

Mark was introduced to the feminist movement by his first wife in the late 1960s. The father of three grown sons, he is now married to his second wife. His family lived in a cooperative community in the 1970s, established by radicals from the free speech movement. He claims to have developed his feminist consciousness by working with feminist women in that community. The men in the community formed men's consciousness-raising groups alongside their female partners' feminist consciousness-raising groups. Mark not only was a feminist activist but was also involved in health politics, the Communist Party, and work for the Black Panthers. He subsequently became involved with profeminist men's groups and was still a profeminist activist at the time of the interview.

Mark's childhood social life was mainly in a Jewish milieu. He was a very active member of his synagogue, even independently of his parents, chanting from the Torah there weekly. In college, his mentor was a liberation theologist whom he credits with raising his political consciousness.

Miriam

Miriam was the youngest person I interviewed. She was a teenager when the second-wave feminist movement began. She reported feeling "disillusioned and disoriented at the loss of the political movements" that she took part in when she was in her twenties. Miriam is an academic who chose to be a single mother at the age of forty. She was involved in Marxist feminist groups after becoming disheartened with the sexism of her Marxist/socialist communities. She dabbled in writing theory. Miriam also spent some time living in women's separatist communities, but she experienced anti-Semitism there, so she left. Miriam has long identified as a writer and artist. She became an academic in the years immediately preceding our interview.

Miriam remembered observing her mother's unhappiness at being a housewife who was dependent on her husband. She also recalled the marginalization of growing up Jewish in a midwestern town: "And people in . . . the Bible Belt, they thought I was a foreigner. But I didn't know why. Because my parents told me we were Americans just like everybody else. So I was raised with a very assimilationist perspective." When she was in her mid-twenties, however, she became a caretaker to her elderly Orthodox grandfather, which sparked her desire to "reconnect with her roots." She learned from her grandfather about the world that she had felt cut off from by her parents, who were trying to assimilate into middle-class Christian America.

Nancy

Nancy, who suffers from mental illness, works as a mental health advocate. She was an activist in the anti–Vietnam War movement at the same time that she was entering the feminist movement. For a while, she lived in a commune with radical activists of all sorts (black nationalists, gay liberationists, Maoists, and others) and became active in various radical groups herself. Later, Nancy became a lesbian separatist. She said that although she enjoyed her political activism, she now realizes that she was mimicking others and that she did not have her "own voice." As a Jew, Nancy felt somewhat at odds with her lesbian feminist community. She was sometimes the target of what she called "reverse classism," when people would equate her with the bourgeoisie because she was Jewish.

Nancy grew up in a small town where hers was the only Jewish family. She was raised with very little Jewish education and recalled her "assimilationist" outlook in childhood with regret. She has become more interested in Judaism as an adult. She belongs to a Reform synagogue, where she is active in communal activities. She married a man later in life and was still married to him at the time of the interview. Although Nancy's interview is not directly quoted in this book, her story informed my analysis.

Naomi

Naomi is one of the older women in the sample and also a veteran of the antiwar and civil rights movements. She still considers herself a peace activist. She is a writer who focuses partly on Jewish women. As a former college professor, she used to send her students to the underground abortion network Jane before abortion was legalized.[9] She has a talent for bringing people together and creating rituals. Even though Naomi is American, she credits herself with having gotten the Israeli feminist movement started when she lived in Israel briefly. She has personally led confrontations with anti-Semitism in the feminist movement and with sexism within institutional Jewish settings.

Like many of the other interviewees, Naomi was raised by a socialist father. She claims that she has always been a Conservative Jew, but for many years she battled with rabbis who would not speak out against the Vietnam War, and then later for feminism. She referred to Judaism as her "home base" and spoke about the ecstasy she feels when she sings in synagogue. She has created many Jewish feminist rituals: "But I feel you can take that base and radicalize it. I'm not a Torah believer. It's a historical mythic text." She credits herself with having encouraged many Jewish feminists to proclaim their own Jewish identities.

Natalie

Natalie is a lawyer who specializes in what she calls "domestic relations" work. She also writes, teaches writing, and is an active volunteer for her synagogue. Natalie is one of the women who said that they would have been rabbis if it had been possible when they were coming of age.[10] "And I had the thought that I would like to be a rabbi. But at that time, there was no such thing as a woman rabbi even in the Reform movement. So I had a very clear idea that I was willing to do something that not very many women did, like be a lawyer. But I could not make that leap of imagination to trying to do something that no woman had done and that was forbidden to women." In the early 1970s, Natalie formed a feminist counseling practice with a group of other women, the first in her city, working on cases such as occupational gender discrimination and joint custody. She was also active in developing rape crisis centers and cooperative daycare programs with gender-neutral curricula.

Natalie grew up in a community with very few Jews and experienced quite a bit of discrimination. Nevertheless, her parents were actively practicing Reform Jews: "All of the closest stuff in my family revolved around being Jewish, and I thought it was terrific . . . So we were always very involved . . . This was our life. Even though I had experienced a lot of discrimination, it didn't make me not want to be Jewish or anything." Natalie has continued the family tradition by taking an active part in the leadership of her synagogue and communal organizing. Earlier in life, however, she struggled to maintain her Jewish practice while raising her children with a Jewish husband who was antagonistic toward Judaism. They later divorced, and she found her own way to practice Judaism. At the time of the interview, Natalie expressed the joy and fulfillment she had found in her Jewish practice.

Olivia

Olivia is a retired professor who still writes and edits women's studies journals. She was a founding member of her local chapter of NOW and participated in some of the earlier second-wave protests, including the well-known demonstration at the Miss American Pageant in 1968.[11] Olivia feels that she suffered negative repercussions for breaking new ground as a professor of women's studies and ethnic studies. She did all of this while raising her children as a single mother. She has taught African American literature and other "ethnic" literature courses for decades, and "I even became Afrocentric in my mind. If you read my first book, you'd think I was a black woman." While Olivia pointed out that the feminists of her generation have been criticized for being essentialists, she maintains that she still feels that patriarchy is the root cause of all oppressions around the globe.

She has been a secular Jew and claims to only recently be "identifying more as a Jew," for a number of reasons: she was critiqued for writing about every other group of women except Jews, she experienced anti-Semitism among her academic peers, and she sees herself as nearing old age. "It wouldn't have happened five years ago that I would be here as a Jew." She is the daughter of Eastern European Jewish immigrants and seems to be extremely worried about anti-Semitism. For instance, she mentioned that she is afraid to open packages addressed to her for fear that they might contain explosives.

Rachel

Like only a few other people I interviewed, Rachel is neither an academic nor working in a nonprofit field. She is an accountant. Rachel identified herself as a religious Jew, commenting that she was aware that not all Jews are. She used more God-language than most of the other people I interviewed. She is very active in a few different synagogues and lives with her lesbian partner of twenty years.

Rachel has struggled with mental health problems throughout her life, and much of her political autobiography is related to the ups and downs of her psychiatric state as well. She was a member of some student protest organizations, including SDS, before she discovered radical feminist groups. Rachel is also one of the few people I interviewed who have ever lived in the South; she spent many of her women's liberation years there. When I asked her to tell me her feminist autobiography, she replied: "It was generally pretty damn chaotic, and the older I get the happier I get, so I'm thinking back on really miserable times. And I don't really want to remember because it sucked." She apparently was in and out of mental institutions, lived on the streets, and was often a drug user. She hopped around from radical community to radical community. Whereas many of the others talked about that time as some of the best years of their lives, Rachel recalled it as a very trying part of her life.

Randi

Randi is a well-known writer, but she does not consider that her greatest accomplishment in life. Being a feminist is her raison d'être: "I certainly was confused before I found the movement, which was at the beginning of the movement—1967. My life felt full of contradiction, which the contradictions were eliminated as soon as I became a feminist . . . And I continued to feel from this moment that that's who I am and that's what my life means, if you will. I mean, that's what I've done with my life." Randi belonged to various local radical feminist groups. In fact, she was a prominent figure in the founding of radical feminism. She even joined the National Organization for Women for a short time, before she realized that "they were not as radical as I wanted to be." Even though the radical feminist groups have long since disbanded, when I asked Randi what kind of feminist she is, she still used a typically radical feminist definition: "I'm a feminist who wants a transformation of society so that gender no longer applies. That's what I want. And anything less than that is the kind of feminist I'm not."

Rebecca

Rebecca is a retired academic who continues to write about gender and feminism. Like many others, she was involved in Vietnam War protests and the civil rights movement. She remembers participating in the march on Washington in 1963.[12] She then became an active feminist, beginning as a liberal feminist (according to her self-definition) protesting workplace discrimination and sexual harassment. She later became more of a socialist feminist, and from there she took a more nuanced theoretical perspective on gender and taught others feminist theory.

Rebecca is not a secular Jew, yet she expressed some ambivalence about her religious practice. She was unaffiliated and secular for many years, and in recent years has become more involved in synagogue life. She raised her child as a single mother, which had a profound influence on her feminist beliefs. She also credits her feminist socialization to her rebellion against the differential treatment that she and her brother received from their parents. She resented the restrictive feminine role that was expected of her, and looks back at her rebellion as a nascent feminism, before she know what feminism was.

Rhonda

Rhonda is another feminist academic, whose political activism began in her childhood and continued through the time of the interview. She explained that she was initially a "left liberal" whose political identity was based entirely on class and race, but she later shifted to become a feminist as well. Her entrée into feminism was through a Marxist-feminist group. These kinds of groups studied together and often collaborated in writing social theory. She participated in the student protest movements of the 1960s against the Vietnam War and for civil rights.

Rhonda's Jewish upbringing was complex. While her father was a secular communist Jew, her mother was Orthodox, and Rhonda observed the Sabbath with her. Rhonda remained religiously observant until she was in graduate school. "So he was communist and my mother was Orthodox," she said. "And I have spent my life trying to put those things together in a very uneven way. Although I think now they've come together for me nicely." Rhonda described herself as "allergic to religion." Yet she also explained that being Jewish suffuses everything she does. She remains involved in Jewish groups, researches Jewish topics, and described her worldview as based in her Jewishness. Rhonda divorced her husband and came out as a lesbian in the 1990s. She has one child.

Rosalyn

Rosalyn did not fit the stereotype of a 1970s feminist—she was a homemaker married to a rabbi. Nevertheless, she became visible in her small town as an outspoken advocate for the Equal Rights Amendment and abortion rights. Rosalyn was president of her local chapter of the National Organization for Women and also served on the state board of the organization. Her methods of activism included organizing demonstrations, responding to the media, and meeting with politicians. She encountered resistance from people in her community, and her husband was pressured to rein in her activism. Nonetheless, Rosalyn was persistent and even ran as a delegate to the Democratic National Convention. She saw her feminist activism as an extension of the mission of Reform Judaism.

Rosalyn was one of the few interviewees who had never identified with the radical feminist mission. In fact, she very clearly defined herself against radical feminism. When I asked her the type of feminist she was not, she answered: "I'm not a bra-burning one. I'm not a civil disobedience person. Of course we've really passed that, haven't we?" She simply thought of herself as a "regular" person who was doing what was necessary in fighting for equal rights.

For instance, Rosalyn recalled a conversation she had with a man in the 1970s who accused her of being "different": "I said, 'I'm not different. I'm a homemaker' . . . I wasn't a hippie. I was always reasonably put together. I don't think you could tell me from the junior league." When I responded, "Right, you weren't part of the radical countercultural movement," she replied, "Exactly. Thank you very much. You put it in good words. I was part of the mainstream." This distinguishes Rosalyn from a majority of the people I interviewed, who identified as radicals.

Sam

Sam is also an academic, and much of his work relates to gender and masculinity. He is the only person I interviewed who is the child of Holocaust survivors, and that is a core facet of his identity. Sam grew up in a neighborhood filled with other Holocaust survivors. Later, he was involved in the founding of the profeminist men's movement as well as the founding of the field of men's studies. Sam has found a "greater commitment to institutional Judaism" as a result of having children later in his life.

Sarah

Sarah was primarily a reproductive rights activist. Reproductive rights were an important issue for both of her parents, and she became interested in the subject before *Roe v. Wade*. She was raised as an observant Conservative Jew and said about her upbringing: "There was a feminist foundation within my Jewish experience that made me open to it, that made me receptive to it. That caused it to strike me powerfully, emotionally." After serving as a leader in major reproductive rights organizations, Sarah went on to become more interested in feminist theory, partly because of her own personal discomfort with dichotomous, simplistic definitions of gender. Although not an academic (she works in the nonprofit sector), she is intellectually engaged with the same topics as women's studies and gender studies professors. Sarah has continued to be an observant Jew and, along with her husband, raised her son in Conservative participatory *minyanim*. Although she is married to a man, she identifies as bisexual. She has struggled to rectify her always evolving notions of gender with her deep love of Judaism.

Steven

Steven has engaged in antiracist activism along with his profeminist work. He writes, gives workshops, and does public speaking engagements on male violence, racism, homophobia, and diversity issues. Steven lives with his female partner and teenage children. His activism in the 1970s began with participation in a workers' collective and led him to profeminist activism around issues of male violence: the battered women's movement, rape prevention, and eventually the founding of a men's center. This was a typical path for the profeminist men in my group. Also, like most of the women, Steven was initially an activist in the civil rights and antiwar movements.

Steven explained that he grew up in a typical American Jewish family without thinking much about being Jewish. Later, after becoming a diversity trainer, he began to examine his Jewish identity in much more depth: "And I think doing the work that we've done in a multicultural environment and working on issues of race and class and gender, it made me, you know, come to grips with what was the complex mix of being Jewish doing this work." Today much of his work takes place in the Jewish community. He has been influential in raising consciousness about violence in the organized Jewish community. He identifies as a practicing Jew. He and his Christian partner are raising their children with both religious identities. Much of our conversation was about his theoretical viewpoints on Jews and race.

Terry

Terry explained that as a red diaper baby, she always had a strong political consciousness. She was also an activist in the civil rights movement. She described her mother as a "great and strong feminist." She also said that when she joined the Communist Party at the age of sixteen, she was educated about male chauvinism. However, she did not identify as a feminist herself until she separated from her husband and joined a consciousness-raising group. Terry became involved in the feminist music scene shortly after that and remains active in it today. She was raised in the Yiddishist/socialist community that some of my other interviewees experienced growing up: "I think you'll probably find that most women who were raised as I was in politically conscious families, red diaper babies like myself . . . have moved into feminism—a logical place to go with that."

Soon after, Terry came out as a lesbian: "And what happened was that being a lesbian . . . that it gave me permission to claim all the different parts of myself, including being Jewish, which I had not really thought of that much. I wasn't raised religious. Obviously our religion was communism. And Yiddish culture was a big part of that." She often substituted the word "lesbian" for "feminist." It seemed like they are interchangeable concepts to her. Feeling vulnerable as a target was a thread throughout her interview, beginning with being born during the Red Scare in a communist family, but also as a Jew and a feminist.

Notes

Introduction

1. Also called the "Wailing Wall," the Western Wall is a remnant of the Second Temple in Jerusalem and a holy site for Jews.

2. What she actually said was, "Dina, turn off the hairdryer! It's Shabbat!" "Shabbat" is the Hebrew term for the Jewish Sabbath. Traditionally, Jews do not use electricity on the Sabbath, which would include the hairdryer.

3. Orthodox Judaism is the most traditional denomination within Judaism. It is, however, made up of communities that fall along a spectrum of Jewish practice. The more stringent adherents of the tradition, such as the ultra-Orthodox, follow different communal norms than the more moderate or "modern Orthodox" Jews. While the teachers of Jewish subjects at my school were all ultra-Orthodox, the most observant students were modern Orthodox, and the rest of us were from every facet of Judaism. The school was hardly a fortress of Orthodox students; one of my fellow students was notorious for bringing ham and cheese sandwiches from home for his lunch—a very big taboo according to Jewish dietary laws.

4. The Conservative movement is considered to be in the middle of Jewish denominations in terms of its perspective on Jewish tradition. The term "egalitarian" has been used to refer to the trend toward allowing girls and women full participation in synagogue leadership: leading services, chanting from the texts in front of the congregation, and becoming b'not-mitzvah. Luckily for me, this trend was already in full swing by the time I attended a Conservative day school in the 1980s.

5. The notion that a photocopied page is distinct from the bound text is certainly strange. I queried my rabbinic friends about this and was not able to find an explanation in Jewish sources for the rabbi's "compromise." In fact, Jewish laws

about learning Talmud predate photocopy machines and the printing press! There is a discussion in the Talmud about teaching women Torah in which Rabbi Eliezer says, "anyone who teaches his daughter Torah teaches her lewdness" (Mishna Sota 3:4). My teacher was following the customs of his Orthodox community, in which girls and women are certainly not encouraged to learn Talmud. Then why agree to teach me from a photocopied page? Perhaps he was interested in working with me but did not want his colleagues to see me carrying around a volume of the Talmud? I really cannot explain it. We never followed through with the plan to study Talmud together, and even if we had, I might not have gotten an explanation from Rabbi S.

6. Selections from the Hebrew Bible are chanted before a congregation three times a week.

7. The term "second wave" is used to refer to the feminist movement of the 1960s and 1970s, while "first wave" refers to the suffrage movement. While this terminology has been criticized for implying that feminism did not exist in the in-between years, I use it for ease of reference to the women's liberation movement of the sixties and seventies.

8. The interviews were carried out over a ten-month period, between August 1999 and June 2000. I chose to conduct oral histories, in which I asked the participants about their earlier life experiences, Jewish upbringing, and women's movement experiences, because of the nature of my topic of study—identity. Since the focus of my analysis is the ways in which people connect the Jewish and feminist aspects of themselves, I felt that a qualitative research method, which lends itself to the discovery of human subjectivity, would be the best way of approaching this research.

9. Since where one lives inevitably affects one's Jewish identity, I interviewed people in various regions of the country. I traveled to the West Coast, Midwest, and Southwest, and I also conducted interviews in the Northeast. Although I lived in New York City at the time, I wanted to interview people who lived outside of this area; the New York City metropolitan area is home to the largest concentration of American Jews, so Jewish identity may be different there. See Bethamie Horowitz, "Why Is This City Different from Other Cities: New York and the 1990 National Jewish Population Survey," *Journal of Jewish Communal Service* 68 (1992): 312–320. In the end, I found that many of my informants had lived in the New York metropolitan area at some point in their lives. Twelve of them were living there at the time of the interview, sixteen had grown up there, and another three had lived there for a period of time during their youths. I did find that the environment one lives in and the concentration of its Jewish population has an influence on one's Jewish identity.

10. See, for example, Gloria Anzaldúa, *Making Face, Making Soul/Haciendo Caras: Creative and Critical Perspectives by Women of Color* (San Francisco: Aunt Lute, 1990); Gloria Anzaldúa et al., *Borderlands/La Frontera: The New Mestiza*

(San Francisco: Aunt Lute, 1987); Patricia Hill Collins, *Black Feminist Thought: Knowledge, Consciousness, and the Politics of Empowerment* (Boston: Unwin Hyman Collins, 1990); bell hooks, *Talking Back: Thinking Feminist, Thinking Black* (Boston: South End Press, 1989); hooks, *Ain't I a Woman? Black Women and Feminism* (Boston: South End Press, 1981); Barbara Smith, *Home Girls: A Black Feminist Anthology* (New York: Kitchen Table Press, 1983); Cherríe Moraga and Gloria Anzaldúa, eds., *This Bridge Called My Back: Writings by Radical Women of Color* (New York: Kitchen Table Press, 1983); Deborah King, "Multiple Jeopardy, Multiple Consciousness: The Context of Black Feminist Ideology," *Signs: Journal of Culture and Society* 14, no. 1 (1988): 42–72.

11. For the argument that feminists have become dogmatic in accusing each other of not paying heed to race, class, and gender, see Susan Bordo, "Feminism, Postmodernism, and Gender Skepticism," in *Feminism/Postmodernism*, ed. Linda Nicholson (New York: Routledge, 1990), 133–156; and Jane Flax, *Disputed Subjects: Essays on Psychoanalysis, Politics and Philosophy* (New York: Routledge, 1993). Flax, ironically, refers to gender, class, and race as the "holy trinity of 'difference'" (5).

12. Martha Ackelsberg, "Toward a Multicultural Politics: A Jewish Feminist Perspective," in *The Narrow Bridge: Jewish Views on Multiculturalism*, ed. Marla Brettschneider (New Brunswick, NJ: Rutgers University Press, 1996), 89–104; David Biale, Michael Galchinsky, and Susannah Heschel, eds., *Insider/Outsider: American Jews and Multiculturalism* (Berkeley: University of California Press, 1998).

13. For examples of autobiographical writing by feminists (of the second-wave generation) in which the author writes about his or her own Jewish identity, see Bella Abzug, "Bella on Bella," *Moment* 1, no. 7 (February 1976): 26–29; Harry Brod, "Introduction," in *A Mensch among Men: Explorations in Jewish Masculinity* (Freedom, CA: Crossing Press, 1988), 1–15; Elly Bulkin, "Hard Ground: Jewish Identity, Racism, and Anti-Semitism," in *Yours in Struggle: Three Feminist Perspectives on Anti-Semitism and Racism,* by Elly Bulkin, Minnie Bruce Pratt, and Barbara Smith (Ithaca, NY: Firebrand Books, 1984), 89–193; Berenice Carroll, "Three Faces of Trevia: Identity, Activism, and Intellect," in *Voices of Women Historians: The Personal, the Political, the Professional,* ed. Eileen Boris and Nupur Chaudhuri (Bloomington: Indiana University Press, 1999), 13–28; Barbara Epstein, "Ambivalence about Feminism," in *The Feminist Memoir Project: Voices from Women's Liberation,* ed. Rachel Blau DuPlessis and Ann Snitow (New York: Three Rivers Press, 1998), 124–148; Betty Friedan, *Life So Far: A Memoir* (New York: Simon and Schuster, 2000); Miriyam Glazer, "'Crazy, of Course': Spiritual Romanticism and the Redeeming of Female Spirituality in Contemporary Jewish-American Women's Fiction," in *People of the Book: Thirty Scholars Reflect on Their Jewish Identity*, ed. Jeffrey Rubin-Dorsky and Shelley Fisher Fishkin (Madison: University of Wisconsin Press, 1996), 439–455; Helen Mayer Hacker, "Slouching

toward Sociology," in *Individual Voices, Collective Visions: Fifty Years of Women in Sociology*, ed. Ann Goetting and Sarah Fenstermaker (Philadelphia: Temple University Press, 1995), 233–250; Karla Jay, *Tales of the Lavender Menace: A Memoir of Liberation* (New York: Basic Books, 1999); Phillipa Kafka, "Preface," in *(Un)doing the Missionary Position: Gender Asymmetry in Contemporary Asian American Women's Writing* (Westport, CT: Greenwood Press, 1997), xiii–xix; Melanie Kaye/Kantrowitz, "Stayed on Freedom: Jew in the Civil Rights Movement and After," in *The Narrow Bridge: Jewish Views on Multiculturalism*, ed. Marla Brettschneider (New Brunswick, NJ: Rutgers University Press, 1996), 105–122; Suzanne Keller, "Bridging Worlds: A Sociologist's Memoir," in Goetting and Fenstermaker, *Individual Voices, Collective Visions*, 151–168; Michael Kimmel, "Judaism, Masculinity and Feminism," in Brod, *A Mensch among Men*, 153–156; Gerda Lerner, "Part I: History as Memory," in *Why History Matters: Life and Thought* (New York: Oxford University Press, 1997), 1–58; Elaine Marks, "'Juifemme,'" in Rubin-Dorsky and Fishkin, *People of the Book*, 343–356; Marge Piercy, *Sleeping with Cats: A Memoir* (New York: Harper, 2002); Riv-Ellen Prell, "Terrifying Tales of Jewish Womanhood," in Rubin-Dorsky and Fishkin, *People of the Book*, 98–114; Adrienne Rich, "Split at the Root," in *Nice Jewish Girls: A Lesbian Anthology*, ed. Evelyn Torton Beck (Boston: Beacon Press, 1989), 73–90; Lillian Rubin, "An Unanticipated Life," in *Gender and the Academic Experience: Berkeley Women Sociologists*, ed. Kathryn Meadow-Orlans and Ruth Wallace (Lincoln: University of Nebraska Press, 1994), 229–247; Alix Kates Shulman, *A Good Enough Daughter* (New York: Schocken Books, 1999); Gaye Tuchman, "Kaddish and Renewal," in Goetting and Fenstermaker, *Individual Voices, Collective Visions*, 303–318; Hannah Schiller Wartenberg, "Obstacles and Opportunities en Route to a Career in Sociology," ibid., 51–66; Ellen Willis, "Next Year in Jerusalem," *Rolling Stone Magazine*, April 1977, 76–80; Bonnie Zimmerman, "The Challenge of Conflicting Communities: To Be Lesbian and Jewish and a Literary Critic," in Rubin-Dorsky and Fishkin, *People of the Book*, 203–216.

14. See, for example, Susan Gubar, "Eating the Bread of Affliction: Judaism and Feminist Criticism," in Rubin-Dorsky and Fishkin, *People of the Book*, 15–36; Nancy Miller, "Hadassah Arms," ibid., 153–168; Zimmerman, "The Challenge of Conflicting Communities."

15. On the prominence of Jewish women in the women's liberation movement, see, for example, Joyce Antler, *The Journey Home: Jewish Women and the American Century* (New York: Free Press, 1997), 260–261; Nathan Glazer, "The Anomalous Liberalism of American Jews," in *The Americanization of the Jews*, ed. Robert Seltzer and Norman Cohen (New York: New York University Press, 1995), 133–143; Moshe Hartman and Harriet Hartman, *Gender Equality and American Jews* (New York: State University of New York Press, 1996), 15–16; Howard Sachar, *A History of the Jews in America* (New York: Vintage Books, 1992), 833–834.

16. Many of my interviewees used the term "coming out of the closet" to describe their newly public Jewish identities.

17. Jews of European descent in America have not always been considered white. For the history of racial construction of American Jews, see Karen Brodkin, *How Jews Became White Folks and What That Says about Race in America* (New Brunswick, NJ: Rutgers University Press, 1998).

18. See, for example, Gubar, "Eating the Bread of Affliction"; Kimmel, "Judaism, Masculinity and Feminism"; Marks, "'Juifemme'"; Miller, "Hadassah Arms."

19. For accounts of anti-Semitism in feminism, see Evelyn Torton Beck, "Why Is This Book Different from All Other Books?" in Beck, *Nice Jewish Girls*, xv–xxxviii; Annette Daum, "Blaming Jews for the Death of the Goddess," *Lilith* 7 (1980): 12–13; Irena Klepfisz, "Anti-Semitism in the Lesbian/Feminist Movement," in Beck, *Nice Jewish Girls*, 51–57; Letty Cottin Pogrebin, "Anti-Semitism in the Women's Movement," *Ms.*, June 1982, 45–49.

20. Lynn Davidman and Shelly Tenenbaum, "Toward a Feminist Sociology of American Jews," in *Feminist Perspectives on Jewish Studies*, ed. Lynn Davidman and Shelly Tenenbaum (New Haven, CT: Yale University Press, 1994), 140–168.

21. For a qualitative sociological study of Jewish feminism in the American Jewish community, see Sylvia Barack Fishman, *A Breath of Life: Feminism in the American Jewish Community* (New York: Free Press, 1993). For qualitative studies of newly Orthodox American women, see the work of sociologists Debra Renee Kaufman, *Rachel's Daughters: Newly Orthodox Jewish Women* (New Brunswick, NJ: Rutgers University Press 1991); and Lynn Davidman, *Tradition in a Rootless World: Women Turn to Orthodox Judaism* (Berkeley: University of California Press, 1991). For ethnographic studies of religious women in Israel, see the works of Israeli anthropologists Tamar El-Or, *Educated and Ignorant: Ultraorthodox Jewish Women and Their World* (Boulder, CO: Lynne Rienner, 1994); and Susan Starr Sered, *Women as Ritual Experts: The Religious Lives of Elderly Jewish Women in Jerusalem* (Oxford, 1992). For explorations of Jewish gender stereotypes and images of Jewish women within popular culture, see Susan Kray, "Orientalization of an 'Almost White' Woman: The Interlocking Effects of Race, Class, Gender, and Ethnicity in American Mass Media," *Cultural Studies in Mass Communication* 10 (1993): 349–366; Riv-Ellen Prell, *Fighting to Become Americans: Gender, Jews, and the Anxiety of Assimilation* (Boston: Beacon Press, 1999); and Gladys Rothbell, "The Jewish Mother: Social Construction of a Popular Image," in *The Jewish Family: Myths and Reality*, ed. Steven M. Cohen and Paula E. Hyman (New York: Holmes and Meier, 1986), 118–122. For a quantitative data analysis comparing American Jewish women to non-Jewish white women and to Jewish men with respect to levels of education, labor force participation, and occupational achievement, see Hartman and Hartman, *Gender Equality and American Jews*.

22. In response to my query, I received between 75 and 100 e-mail messages. The volume of responses surprised me, because I had been taught that it is difficult to persuade people to participate in social research. Instead, I found people to be extremely enthusiastic and interested in the topic of my study. Their responses helped convince me that there is a need for research on Jewish second-wave femi-

nists. My initial query was forwarded by e-mail to such an extent that many of the people who contacted me did not know where it originated. Also, of the people with whom I made initial contact, who either had been recommended to me or identified themselves as Jewish second-wave feminists in their writing, only a handful refused to be interviewed.

23. I did interview a few people like this, because I did not realize prior to the interview that although they identified as second-wave feminists, they had not really been involved in the feminist movement; their affiliation with feminism was only by identification. I knew after those particular interviews were finished and they had described their lives in the 1960s and 1970s without mentioning any overt social movement participation that I could not include them in the study. I also interviewed a couple of people who, though they had taken part in feminist activities, identified themselves not as feminists but rather as social activists of other kinds. I omitted them from my analysis as well, because I wanted to narrow the sample down to people with feminist identities who had participated in second-wave feminism.

24. As was common for second-wave feminists, many of my informants became academics. In fact, twelve were academics at the time of the interviews. All of the academics whom I interviewed have engaged in feminist scholarship and have made gender a primary area of their work. Most of the others work in the nonprofit sector. Moreover, almost all of the interviewees were writers in some capacity; if not academics or writers by profession, they wrote articles, poems, or essays for pleasure. As a group, the informants' intelligence, eloquence, and thoughtfulness come through in the interview accounts.

25. For more information on this research method, see Michael V. Angrosino, *Documents of Interaction: Biography, Autobiography, and Life History in Social Science Perspective* (Gainesville: University Press of Florida, 1989); Robert Atkinson, *The Life Story Interview: Qualitative Research Methods V* (Thousand Oaks, CA: Sage Publications, 1998); Amia Lieblich et al., *Narrative Research: Reading, Analysis, and Interpretation* (Thousand Oaks, CA: Sage Publications, 1998); Catherine Kohler Riessman, *Narrative Analysis* (Thousand Oaks, CA: Sage Publications, 1993); Valerie Raleigh Yow, *Recording Oral History: A Practice Guide for Social Scientists* (Thousand Oaks, CA: Sage Publications, 1994).

26. All interviews were tape-recorded and transcribed. I then coded the transcripts for key themes, using the NVivo qualitative data analysis software program. The main category of analysis for this study is intersections between Jewishness and feminism. I selected all material pertaining to both gender/feminism and Judaism/Jewish identity/Jewish experiences; my analysis of the resulting narratives was the basis for the organization of the data.

27. Russell Bernard, *Research Methods in Anthropology: Qualitative and Quantitative Approaches,* 2nd ed. (Walnut Creek, CA: AltaMira Press, 1995); Herbert J. Rubin and Irene S. Rubin, *Qualitative Interviewing: The Art of Hearing Data*

(Newbury Park, CA: Sage Publications, 1995); Stephen J. Taylor, *Introduction to Qualitative Research Methods: A Guidebook and Resource* (New York: John Wiley and Sons, 1998).

28. Jennifer C. Hunt, *Psychoanalytic Aspects of Fieldwork,* vol. 18 (Newbury Park, CA: Sage Publications, 1989); and Catherine Kohler Riessman, "When Gender Is Not Enough: Women Interviewing Women," *Gender and Society* 1 (1987): 172–307.

29. A group of interviewees, including Ann, Rhonda, Naomi, and Eleanor, identified themselves as "red diaper babies," meaning that they were raised in socialist or communist families. Many Jewish immigrants were active in the labor movement and formed Yiddishist/socialist communities during the first half of the twentieth century.

30. These groups focus on issues such as *agunot,* "chained women" whose husbands refuse to grant them Jewish divorces. See, for example, the Jewish Orthodox Feminist Alliance, http://www.jofa.org. For more modern Orthodox feminist perspectives, see Blu Greenberg, *On Women and Judaism: A View from Tradition* (Philadelphia: Jewish Publication Society, 1981).

Note: When a hyphen is used in "Jewish-feminist" or "Jewish-feminism," it indicates activism that was focused within the Jewish community.

31. Alba, *Ethnic Identity: The Transformation of White America* (New Haven, CT: Yale University Press, 1990), 50.

32. Walker Connor, in writing about the murkiness of the concept of nationality, uses the example of Freud's reflections about his own Jewish identity: "After noting that he was Jewish, Freud made clear that his own sense of Jewishness had nothing to do with either religion or national pride. He went on to note that he was 'irresistibly' bonded to Jews and Jewishness by 'many obscure and emotional forces, which were the more powerful the less they could be expressed in words, as well as by a clear consciousness of inner identity, a deep realization of sharing the same psychic structure.'" Connor, "Beyond Reason: The Nature of Ethnonational Bond," reprinted in *Ethnicity,* ed. John Hutchinson and Anthony D. Smith (Oxford: Oxford University Press, 1996), 72.

33. I use the term "Jewishness" instead of "Judaism" because "Judaism" is more limited in connotation to the Jewish religion, whereas "Jewishness" encompasses culture or ethnicity as well.

34. Horowitz, "The Paradox of Jewish Studies in the New Academy," in Biale, Galchinsky, and Haschel, *Insider/Outsider,* 125. For more on global Jewish identities, see Caryn Aviv and David Shneer, *New Jews: The End of the Jewish Diaspora* (New York: NYU Press, 2005).

35. Nathan Glazer, *American Judaism* (Chicago: University of Chicago Press, 1957); Paula Hyman, *Gender and Assimilation in Modern Jewish History: The Roles and Representations of Women* (Seattle: University of Washington Press, 1995); Sachar, *A History of the Jews in America.*

36. Sara Bershtel and Allen Graubard, *Saving Remnants: Feeling Jewish in America* (New York: Free Press, 1992); Hartman and Hartman, *Gender Equality and American Jews;* Seymour Martin Lipset and Earl Raab, *Jews and the New American Scene* (Cambridge, MA: Harvard University Press, 1995).

37. Hartman and Hartman, *Gender Equality and American Jews.*

38. For histories of feminism, see Sara Evans, *Personal Politics: The Roots of Women's Liberation in the Civil Rights Movement and the New Left* (New York: Vintage, 1979); and Ruth Rosen, *The World Split Open: How the Modern Women's Movement Changed America* (New York: Penguin Books, 2000).

39. The publication of *The Feminine Mystique* was said to have turned many a housewife on to feminism. When I asked Edith how she got involved in NOW and feminist activities, she replied, "I can tell you exactly where I was when I read *The Feminist Mystique* [sic]. Was very simple, was on my bed, with a mild case of depression, absolutely wanting something else. I was the classic upper-middle-class Jewish person that Betty Friedan was writing about. And so that kind of feminism was created for me. I began to try to redefine who I was . . . Until then it had been a silent rebellion, from not having voice and determination in my life. So that was how I got identified with feminism."

40. Naomi Shepherd, *A Price below Rubies: Jewish Women as Rebels and Radicals* (Cambridge, MA: Harvard University Press, 1993).

41. The Pale of Settlement comprised the provinces of the Russian Empire to which Jews were confined between 1722 and 1917; ibid., 7.

42. Susan A. Glenn, *Daughters of the Shtetl: Life and Labor in the Immigrant Generation* (Ithaca, NY: Cornell University Press, 1990); Shepherd, *A Price below Rubies.*

43. Linda Gordon Kuzmack, *Woman's Cause: The Jewish Woman's Movement in England and the United States, 1881–1933* (Columbus: Ohio State University Press, 1990).

44. Fishman, *A Breath of Life;* Susannah Heschel, ed., *On Being a Jewish Feminist* (New York: Schocken Books, 1983); Lerner, "Part I: History as Memory."

45. Blessing the Torah, or having an *aliyah* in front of the congregation, is an honored role that women were previously banned from taking part in. Rabbis justified this prohibition by citing the "honor of the congregation."

46. Jack Wertheimer, *Conservative Synagogues and Their Members: Highlights of the North American Survey of 1995–96* (New York: Jewish Theological Seminary of America, 1996).

47. Laurie Goodstein, "Ordained as Rabbis, Women Tell Secret," *New York Times,* December 21, 2000; Goodstein, "Unusual, but Not Unorthodox; Causing a Stir, 2 Synagogues Hire Women to Assist Rabbis," ibid., February 6, 1998; and Michael Luo, "An Orthodox Jewish Woman, and Soon, a Spiritual Leader," ibid., August 21, 2006.

48. Robert Gordis, *The Dynamics of Judaism: A Study of Jewish Law* (Bloomington: Indiana University Press, 1990).

49. A classic example of Jewish legal change in response to social need is the *prozbul* implemented by Rabbi Hillel in which he ruled against the biblical mandate of canceling debts after seven years, because people had stopped lending money, and thus poor people were unable to borrow money; see Marcus Jastrow, *Sefer Milim: A Dictionary of the Targumim, the Talmud Babli and Yerushalmi, and the Midrashic Literature* (New York: Judaica Press, 1996), vol. 1, 1218. Another example is the eleventh-century rabbinic ban on polygyny because of pressure from the church and governments where Jews resided as well as resistance from Jewish women; see Rachel Adler, *Engendering Judaism: An Inclusive Theology and Ethics* (Philadelphia: Jewish Publication Society, 1998), 235 n. 29.

50. Judith Hauptman, *Rereading the Rabbis: A Woman's Voice* (Boulder, CO: Westview Press, 1998).

51. For more on the distinction between these two groups, see Laura Levitt, "Feminist Spirituality," in *Spirituality and the Secular Quest*, ed. Peter H. Van Ness (New York: Crossroad Publishing, 1996).

52. An interesting exception to the religious Jewish-feminist versus secular Jewish feminist dichotomy can be found in the works of secular Jewish women who explored the implications of their *secular* Jewish feminist identities. See, for example, Melanie Kaye/Kantrowitz and Irena Klepfisz, eds., *The Tribe of Dina: A Jewish Women's Anthology*, Revised and Expanded Edition (Boston: Beacon Press, 1986); and Beck, *Nice Jewish Girls*.

53. Fishman, *A Breath of Life*, 2.

Chapter One

1. There are many gay and lesbian synagogues around the country. Rachel referred to her synagogue as a "queer synagogue" because inclusiveness of transgender people is also part of its mission. For an ethnographic study of New York City's gay and lesbian synagogue, see Moshe Shokeid, *A Gay Synagogue in New York* (Philadelphia: University of Pennsylvania Press, 1995).

2. Adler, *Engendering Judaism;* Fishman, *A Breath of Life;* Susan Grossman and Rivka Haut, eds., *Daughters of the King: Women and the Synagogue* (Philadelphia: Jewish Publication Society, 1992); Judith Plaskow, *Standing Again at Sinai* (San Francisco: Harper and Row, 1979).

3. The Conservative movement is the only denomination other than Orthodox that still has some nonegalitarian synagogues. According to Wertheimer's 1996 study, approximately 80 percent of Conservative synagogues were egalitarian; in the years since then, surely more have become egalitarian. See Wertheimer, *Conservative Synagogues and Their Members*, 16.

4. El-Or, *Educated and Ignorant*.

5. Davidman and Tanenbaum, *Feminist Perspectives on Jewish Studies*.

6. For feminist interpretations of Jewish texts, see Hauptman, *Rereading the Rabbis;* Naomi Mara Hyman, ed., *Biblical Women in the Midrash: A Sourcebook* (Northvale, NJ: Jason Aronson, 1997); and Ilana Pardes, *Countertraditions in the*

Bible: A Feminist Approach (Cambridge, MA: Harvard University Press, 1992). For Jewish-feminist theology, see Adler, *Engendering Judaism*; and Plaskow, *Standing Again at Sinai*. For gender-inclusive liturgy, see Marcia Falk, *The Book of Blessing: New Jewish Prayers for Daily Life, the Sabbath, and the New Moon Festival* (Boston: Beacon Press, 1996). For feminist rituals, see Penina Adelman, *Miriam's Well: Rituals for Jewish Women around the Year* (New York: Biblio Press, 1990); Susan Berrin, ed., *Celebrating the New Moon: A Rosh Chodesh Anthology* (Northvale, NJ: Jason Aronson, 1996); E. M. Broner, *Bringing Home the Light: A Jewish Woman's Handbook of Rituals* (San Francisco: Council Oak Books, 1999); Debra Orenstein, ed., *Lifecycles,* vol. 1: *Jewish Women on Life Passages and Personal Milestones* (New York: Jewish Lights, 1994).

7. Sered, *Women as Ritual Experts,* 66.

8. Fishman, *A Breath of Life,* 182–199.

9. Edith remarked that her struggle with the tradition is what progressive rabbi Arthur Waskow calls "Godwrestling." In *Godwrestling* (New York: Schocken, 1987), Waskow claims that questioning is central to Jewish tradition. The book's title is a poetic translation of the word *Yisrael* (Hebrew for Israel), an ancient name for the Jewish people.

10. *Chavurah* is Hebrew for "fellowship." It is a collectively organized prayer and study community. The *chavurah* movement emerged out of the New Left to create an alternative organization to the synagogue. See Riv-Ellen Prell, *Prayer and Community: The Havurah in American Judaism* (Detroit: Wayne State University Press, 1989).

11. Lorber, *Gender Inequality: Feminist Theories and Politics,* 3rd ed. (Los Angeles: Roxbury Press, 2005), 26–44.

12. Pamela Nadell, "The Women Who Would Be Rabbis," in *American Jewish Women's History: A Reader,* ed. Pamela Nadell (New York: NYU Press, 2003), 176.

13. In Jewish communal parlance, a "participatory" congregation is one in which the congregants themselves, rather than a cantor, lead services and chant Torah.

14. *Haftarah* refers to selections, usually from the book of Prophets, that are chanted in synagogue on the Sabbath and holidays.

15. The *bimah* is a platform that acts as a stage.

16. *Simchas Torah* means literally "Celebration of the Torah." During this holiday, the yearly cycle of reading the Torah ends and begins again. Congregants sing, dance, and carry the Torah scrolls around. Traditionally, women did not dance with or carry Torah scrolls.

17. There is a burgeoning feminist movement among Orthodox Jewish women. The Jewish Orthodox Feminist Alliance is a notable organization; see http://www.jofa.org. For more on the conflicts between Orthodox Judaism and feminism, see Greenberg, *On Women and Judaism*; and Tamar Ross, *Expanding the Palace of Torah: Orthodoxy and Feminism* (Lebanon, NH: University Press of New England, 2004).

18. The organization Advancing Women Professionals and the Jewish Community is dedicated to elevating more women into leadership positions in the Jewish philanthropies. See http://www.advancingwomen.org.

19. Alice Echols, *Daring to Be Bad: Radical Feminism in America, 1967–1975* (Minneapolis: University of Minnesota Press, 1989); and Barbara A. Crow, ed., *Radical Feminism: A Documentary Reader* (New York: New York University Press, 2000).

20. Also, the feminist deconstruction of religious texts is an ongoing project of Jewish feminist theologians. The works of Jewish feminist scholars reflect the same tensions presented here between preserving tradition (such as Adler's *Engendering Judaism* or Hauptman's *Rereading the Rabbis*) and challenging the basic assumptions of texts (such as the work of Judith Plaskow).

21. Lorber, *Gender Inequality,* 131.

22. For more on heterosexism within Jewish history and explorations of nonheterosexual Jewish identities, see Rebecca Alpert, *Like Bread on the Seder Plate: Jewish Lesbians and the Transformation of Tradition* (New York: Columbia University Press, 1997); David Schneer and Caryn Aviv, *Queer Jews* (New York: Routledge, 2002); Christie Balka and Andy Rose, eds., *Twice Blessed: On Being Lesbian, Gay, and Jewish* (New York: Beacon Press, 1989); Beck, *Nice Jewish Girls;* and Rebecca Alpert, Sue Levi Elwell, and Shirley Idelson, eds., *Lesbian Rabbis: The First Generation* (New Brunswick, NJ: Rutgers University Press, 2001).

23. Plaskow, "Jewish Theology in Feminist Perspective," in Davidman and Tenenbaum, *Feminist Perspectives on Jewish Studies,* 78.

24. Women of the Wall is an organization that has been fighting for the right of women to lead their own services at the Western Wall in Jerusalem. Phyllis Chesler and Rivka Haut, eds., *Women of the Wall: Claiming Sacred Ground at Judaism's Holy Site* (Woodstock, VT: Jewish Lights Publishing, 2002).

25. The *Kaddish* seems to have been pivotal in creating Jewish-feminists. This prayer, which is said in memory of immediate relatives after their death, has deep symbolic and emotional significance. Many women have reported that a galvanizing moment for them was when they were barred from saying *Kaddish* for a parent because of their gender. See E. M. Broner, *Mornings and Mourning: A Kaddish Journal* (San Francisco: Harper Collins, 1994); Fishman, *A Breath of Life,* 138–141; and Sara Reguer, "Kaddish from the 'Wrong' Side of the *Mehitza,*" in Heschel, *On Being a Jewish Feminist* 177–181.

Chapter Two

1. Jack Rosenfeld, "On Building a Secular Jewish Life," *Jewish Currents,* June 2001, 14–16; Mitchell Silver, *Respecting the Wicked Child: A Philosophy of Secular Jewish Identity and Education* (Amherst: University of Massachusetts Press, 1998).

2. Goodman, *The Faith of Secular Jews* (New York: Ktav Publishing House, 1976), 37.

3. See Levitt, "Impossible Assimilations, American Liberalism, and Jewish Difference: Revisiting Jewish Secularism," *American Quarterly* 59, no. 3 (2007): 802–832; and Levitt, "Feminist Spirituality."

4. According to some estimates, secular-identified Jews make up nearly half of American Jews. See Egon Mayer, Barry A. Kosmin, and Ariela Keysar, *American Jewish Identity Survey 2001: AJIS Report—An Exploration in the Demography and Outlook of a People* (New York: Graduate Center of the City University of New York, 2002), http://www.gc.cuny.edu/faculty/research_studies/ajis.pdf.

5. Goodman, *The Faith of Secular Jews.*

6. Shmuel Feiner, "The Pseudo-Enlightenment and the Question of Jewish Modernization," *Jewish Social Studies* 3 (1996): 62–88.

7. Steven M. Cohen and Arnold M. Eisen, *The Jew Within: Self, Family, and Community in America* (Bloomington: Indiana University Press, 2000), 31.

8. Feiner, "The Pseudo-Enlightenment and the Question of Jewish Modernization"; Goodman, *The Faith of Secular Jews;* Seth Kulick, "The Evolution of Secular Judaism," *Humanist* 53 (1993): 32–36.

9. See http://www.culturaljudaism.org/.

10. See http://www.shj.org.

11. See http://www.csjo.org/pages/about.htm.

12. Neil Gillman, *Sacred Fragments: Recovering Theology for the Modern Jew* (Philadelphia: Jewish Publication Society, 1990), xx.

13. Waskow, *Godwrestling.*

14. Marks, "'Juifemme,'" 346.

15. *Hagaddah* is the text of the traditional Passover service that takes place at home, called a *seder.*

16. Brodsky, "A Way of Being a Jew; a Way of Being a Person," in *Jewish Identity,* ed. David Theo Goldberg and Michael Krausz (Philadelphia: Temple University Press, 1993), 247.

17. This point is similar to feminist standpoint theory, which claims that women have a vision of social relations that is unavailable to men because men benefit from sexism. According to this theory, material life structures knowledge so that the standpoint of the oppressed group exposes the reality of social relations, since it is an inversion of the ruling group's presumptions. See Collins, *Black Feminist Thought;* and Nancy Hartsock, "The Feminist Standpoint: Developing the Ground for a Specifically Feminist Historical Materialism," in *Feminism and Methodology,* ed. Sandra Harding (Bloomington: Indiana University Press, 1987). The interviewees in this book are essentially articulating a Jewish feminist standpoint theory.

18. Bella Abzug was a prominent feminist in the seventies, a New York congresswoman, and leader of the House antiwar movement (*Columbia Encyclopedia,* 6th ed., 2001). For her own discussion of the roots of her activism in her Jewishness, see Abzug, "Bella on Bella."

Chapter Three

1. Sara R. Horowitz discusses the marginalization of Jewish studies within the academy and the invisibility of Jewishness as an "othered" category in "The Paradox of Jewish Studies in the New Academy."

2. Staub, *The Jewish 1960s: An American Sourcebook* (Waltham, MA: Brandeis University Press, 2004), xv–xvi.

3. For a discussion of anti-Semitism in the New Left, see Michael Lerner, *The Socialism of Fools: Anti-Semitism on the Left* (Oakland, CA: Tikkun, 1992).

4. Pegueros, "Radical Feminists—No Jews Need Apply," *Nashim: A Journal of Jewish Women's Studies & Gender Issues* 8 (Fall 2004): 178.

5. Beck, *Nice Jewish Girls*, xxi.

6. Klepfisz, "Anti-Semitism in the Lesbian/Feminist Movement," ibid., 52.

7. Ibid., 53.

8. Pegueros, "Radical Feminists—No Jews Need Apply," 176.

9. Ibid.

10. I want to thank Caryn Aviv for pointing out, in her review of this manuscript, that an overdetermined emphasis on oppression in academic feminism can sometimes overshadow more constructive ways of theorizing feminism that would call for an active role for women as social change agents.

11. Miller, "Hadassah Arms," 161.

12. Joyce Antler, *The Journey Home: Jewish Women and the American Century* (New York: Free Press, 1997), 260, 276; Miriyam Glazer, "'Crazy, of Course': Spiritual Romanticism and the Redeeming of Female Spirituality in Contemporary Jewish-American Women's Fiction," in Rubin-Dorsky and Fishkin, *People of the Book*, 442–443.

13. Glazer, "'Crazy, of Course.'"

14. Pogrebin, "Anti-Semitism in the Women's Movement," 46.

15. Ellen Cantarow, "Zionism, Anti-Semitism and Jewish Identity in the Women's Movement," *Middle East Report* 154 (Sept.–Oct. 1988): 38.

16. Ibid.; Pogrebin, "Anti-Semitism in the Women's Movement"; and Regina Schreiber, "Copenhagen: One Year Later," *Lilith* 8 (1981): 30–35.

17. Schreiber, "Copenhagen: One Year Later."

18. Ibid.

19. Ibid.

20. Babylonian Talmud: Shavuot 39a.

21. See, for instance, bell hooks, *Feminist Theory: From Margin to Center*, 2nd ed. (New York: Pluto Press, 2000).

Chapter Four

1. The term "profeminist" is used to distinguish men from women feminists, in acknowledgment of their different social positions. See Michael Kimmel and

Thomas Mosmiller, *Against the Tide: Pro-feminist Men in the United States, 1776–1990—A Documentary History* (Boston: Beacon Press, 1992).

2. Ibid.; Michael Messner, *Politics of Masculinities: Men in Movements* (Thousand Oaks, CA: Sage Publications, 1997); Messner, "Radical Feminist and Socialist Feminist Men's Movements in the United States," in *Feminism and Men: Reconstructing Gender Relations,* ed. Steven P. Schacht and Doris W. Ewing (New York: NYU Press, 1998), 67–85.

3. R. W. Connell, "Gender Politics for Men," in Schacht and Ewing, *Feminism and Men,* 225–236; Michael Messner, "The Limits of 'The Male Sex Role': An Analysis of the Men's Liberation and Men's Rights Movements' Discourse," *Gender & Society* 12 (1998): 255–276.

4. Tim Carrigan, Bob Connell, and John Lee, "Toward a New Sociology of Masculinity," *Theory and Society* 14 (1985): 551–604.

5. Connell, *Gender and Power: Society, the Person and Sexual Politics* (Stanford, CA: Stanford University Press 1987), 183.

6. Mike Donaldson, "What Is Hegemonic Masculinity?" *Theory and Society* 22 (1993): 643–657.

7. Sharon R. Bird, "Welcome to the Men's Club: Homosociality and the Maintenance of Hegemonic Masculinity," *Gender and Society* 10 (1996): 120–132; Anthony Chen, "Lives at the Center of the Periphery, Lives at the Periphery of the Center: Chinese American Masculinities and Bargaining with Hegemony," *Gender and Society* 13 (1999): 584–607; Donaldson, "What Is Hegemonic Masculinity?"

8. Yen Le Espiritu, "Ideological Racism and Cultural Resistance," in *Asian American Women and Men: Labor, Laws, and Love* (Thousand Oaks, CA: Sage Publications, 1997); Collins, *Black Feminist Thought.*

9. A number of scholars have written about the construction of American Jewish men's masculinity. In *Fighting to Become Americans,* Riv-Ellen Prell details the history of stereotypes of Jewish women and attributes those stereotypes to Jewish men, who she claims projected their anxieties about their ethnic difference onto Jewish women. In "The Sexual Politics of Jewish Identity," chapter 4 of *Gender and Assimilation in Modern Jewish History,* Paula Hyman writes that the modern militaristic Israeli male mentality is a result of years of emasculating Jewish oppression in Europe.

10. Elsie Martel, "From Mensch to Macho?" *Men and Masculinities* 3 (2001): 351.

11. Sander Gilman, *The Jew's Body* (New York: Routledge, 1991); Elliott Horowitz, "The Vengeance of the Jews Was Stronger Than Their Avarice: Modern Historians and the Persian Conquest of Jerusalem in 614," *Jewish Social Studies* 4, no. 2 (1998): 2.

12. Daniel Boyarin, *Unheroic Conduct: The Rise of Heterosexuality and the Invention of the Jewish Man* (Berkeley: University of California Press, 1997), 4.

13. Rosenberg, "A Jewish Men's Movement," in Brod, *A Mensch among Men*, 157.

14. Boyarin, *Unheroic Conduct*, 5.

15. Ibid., 2.

16. Ibid.

17. Ibid., 12.

18. Daniel is referring to a verse in daily morning prayers, "Blessed are you, God, for not having made me a woman," which has been removed from Conservative, Reform, and Reconstructionist prayer books.

19. It is unclear which rabbi he is referring to. It is likely that he means Beruria, who was the daughter of Hananya Ben Teradion, a teacher in second-century Galilee, and the wife of Rabbi Meir, one of the main rabbis of the *Mishna*. See Judith Z. Abrams, *The Women of the Talmud* (Northvale, NJ: Jason Aronson, 1995), 2.

Appendix

1. For more information on "red diaper babies," see Judy Kaplan and Linn Shapiro, *Red Diapers: Growing Up in the Communist Left* (Urbana: University of Illinois Press, 1998); and James Laxer, *Red Diaper Baby: A Boyhood in the Age of McCarthyism* (Vancouver, BC: Douglas & McIntyre, 2004).

2. The hypocrisy of sexism within New Left movements is one of the explanations given for the formation of radical feminist groups. For more information, see Jo Freeman, "The Origins of the Women's Liberation Movement," *American Journal of Sociology* 78, no. 4 (1973): 798–802. See also "Chronology," in DuPlessis and Snitow, *The Feminist Memoir Project*, 497–512.

3. The National Organization for Women (NOW) was founded in 1966, with Betty Friedan serving as its first president through 1970. See DuPlessis and Snitow, *The Feminist Memoir Project*, 498. NOW was seen as the quintessential organization of the liberal feminist branch of the movement, serving as a bureaucratically structured national body, in contrast to the small grassroots collectives typical of radical feminist organizing.

4. Redstockings was one of the original radical feminist groups, founded in February 1969 by Ellen Willis and Shulamith Firestone. They were committed to both political action and consciousness-raising and were best known for their efforts toward repealing abortion laws. For more information, see Echols, *Daring to Be Bad*, 139–158.

5. SDS was founded in 1960 as the youth group of the Old Left social-democratic group LID (League for Industrial Democracy). SDS eventually became more radical than the LID, with an anti-anticommunist perspective. It organized multiracial groups of young activists on racial and economic issues, eventually taking on the Vietnam War as well. It dissolved in 1969. See Echols, *Daring to Be Bad*, 24–25; and Doug McAdam, *Freedom Summer* (New York: Oxford University Press, 1988), 22.

6. On August 26, 1970, some 50,000 activists marched down Fifth Avenue to rally on behalf of Women's Strike for Equality Day, called by Betty Friedan of NOW. It was meant to mark the fiftieth anniversary of women's suffrage and received enormous attention from the press and politicians. See Susan Brownmiller, *In Our Time: Memoir of a Revolution* (New York: Random House, 1999), 146–147.

7. WITCH (Women's International Conspiracy from Hell), formed in 1968, was an offshoot of the New York Radical Women group. For more information, see Echols, *Daring to Be Bad,* 76–80.

8. According to Max Elbaum, there were hundreds of these Marxist study groups around the country; they were often informal, consisting of a small number of young activists who joined together to study the works of Marx, Lenin, and Mao. See Elbaum, *Revolution in the Air: Sixties Radicals Turn to Lenin, Mao and Che* (New York: Verso, 2002), 93–94.

9. Jane evolved out of the Chicago Women's Liberation movement. Originally it was a counseling and referral service for women seeking abortions. However, Jane activists eventually trained women to conduct abortions themselves, and it became one of the safest and cheapest routes for obtaining abortions between 1969 and 1973. For more information, see Jane, "Women Learn to Perform Abortion," in *Dear Sisters: Dispatches from the Women's Liberation Movement,* ed. Rosalyn Baxandall and Linda Gordon (New York: Basic Books, 2000), 145–147.

10. Nadell, "The Women Who Would Be Rabbis."

11. The Miss America protest in September 1968 was one of the most notorious events of the women's liberation movement. During the demonstration, feminists burned symbols of sexism, such as brooms, mops, and bras. For more information, see Echols, *Daring to Be Bad,* 92–101.

12. It was during the August 28, 1963, March on Washington, organized by activists in the civil rights movement, that Dr. Martin Luther King Jr. delivered his "I Have a Dream" speech. For more information, see DuPlessis and Snitow, *The Feminist Memoir Project,* 497.

Index

Abortion rights. *See* Reproductive rights
Abzug, Bella, 55
Activism, defined, 35. *See also* Anti–Vietnam War movement; Civil rights movement; Feminism; Labor movement and labor unions; Social justice
African American studies, 71. *See also* Multiculturalism
Alice (research subject), 40–42, 99
Ann (research subject), 49, 54–55, 99–100, 121n29
Anti-Semitism: in American Left, 66, 67; in Europe, 13, 14, 83, 84; internalized, 53–54, 66, 68, 71, 78, 92–93; and Jewish second-wave feminists, 6, 19, 56, 62–63, 65–79, 101, 102, 106, 107; and stereotypes of Jewish men, 83, 89–90, 128n9; and the United States, 13, 14, 59, 61, 66–79, 101, 102, 109. *See also* Holocaust; Persecution
Anti–Vietnam War movement, 11–12; as motivator for women's groups, 15; participants in, 35, 63, 99, 100, 102, 103, 107, 110, 112
Anti-Zionism, 19, 75, 79
Assimilation, 63, 66–67, 90, 92, 96, 107
Atheism among some Jews, 1, 22, 31, 46, 47. *See also* Religion: opposition to

Barbara (research subject), 55–56, 100
Bat-mitzvah, 26, 27, 29, 103, 105

Battered women's shelters, 11, 81, 99, 101, 112
Biographical sketches of research subjects, 7, 20, 99–113
Brenda (research subject), 100
Bund (Jewish socialist party), 16, 45

Camps, Jewish, 45, 58, 103
Cantors, 16, 27
Catholicism, 57
Center for Cultural Judaism, 45
Chanukah, 47, 56
Chavurah, 26, 124n10
Christianity, 46, 57, 62
Circumcision, 86
Civil rights movement, 15, 56, 58; feminists' involvement in, 11–12, 35, 63, 99–104, 107, 110, 112
Class: characteristics of middle, 91; of contemporary American Jews, 14, 55, 61, 66–69, 88, 107; as division in feminist movement, 5, 61, 62; and intersectionality, 5, 11, 70, 97; markers of, 94; in Marxist feminism, 15, 105, 110; of second-wave feminists, 5, 7, 83, 92, 97, 101; socialists on, 54
"Click moments," defined, 37, 72
Cognitive dissonance. *See under* Feminism (second-wave)
Communal (collective) discourses, 50–51,

54–56, 58, 59. *See also* Cultural discourses

Communism, 54–58, 63, 99–100, 105, 106, 110, 112, 121n29; as form of religion, 57, 113

Communities: comfort found in Jewish, 21–22, 32, 33; impact of, on individual identity construction, 4, 96; Jewish, as supporting women, 85–87; Jewish feminists as bringing change to Jewish, 16, 17–18, 21–42, 91–92, 97; plurality of Jewish, 14. *See also* Communal (collective) discourses

Congress of Secular Jewish Organizations (CSJO), 45, 46

Consciousness-raising, 11, 15, 16, 74, 103, 104, 112; Jewishness not examined in, 64–65; and Jewish textual study, 25; male, 81, 106

Conservative Judaism, 14, 26, 52, 85, 107, 111–112, 115n4; and gender equality, 1–2, 16–17, 26, 30, 32, 123n3

CSJO (Congress of Secular Jewish Organizations), 45, 46

Cultural discourses, 7, 11, 14, 94, 96, 98. *See also* Communal (collective) discourses

Daniel (research subject), 85–87, 89, 90, 92, 93, 101

Discourses: communal, 50–51, 54–56, 58, 59; cultural, 7, 11, 81, 82, 94, 96, 98; of Jewish alternative masculinity, 19, 80–94; of Jewish-feminist congruence, 19, 43, 51, 55, 57, 58–59, 80, 93–94; of Jewishness, 53–54; of multiculturalism, 14, 71, 79, 97

Dissent. *See* Questioning

Domestic violence. *See* Violence against women

Edith (research subject), 24–25, 101, 122n39

Education (general): of American Jewish women, 14, 41, 85–86, 108, 115n5; of research subjects, 7; as valued by Jews, 55. *See also* Education (Jewish); Questioning

Education (Jewish), 89; secular, 45; for women, 1–2, 8, 17, 23, 24–26, 30–31, 34. *See also* Hebrew language

"Egalitarian," 115n4

Eleanor (research subject), 47, 56–57, 102, 121n29

Equal Rights Amendment (ERA), 11, 81, 103, 111

Ethics. *See* Social justice

Ethics of the Fathers, 34

Ethnic studies, 5, 65–66, 71, 108–109. *See also* Jewish studies; Multiculturalism

Europe, 13, 14, 16, 45, 83, 84. *See also* Holocaust

Evelyn (research subject), 47, 49, 53, 56, 102

Feminine Mystique, The (Friedan), 12, 14, 122n39

Feminism (first-wave), 15, 116n7

Feminism (second-wave): academic, 11, 35, 70, 120n24, 127n1 (*see also* Women's studies); and civil rights movement, 11–12, 35, 63, 99–104, 107, 110, 112; cognitive dissonance between Judaism and, 2, 10, 18, 19, 30–42, 44, 48–50, 59, 78, 91–92; as contested identity category, 4, 11; definitions of, 47–48, 54, 80, 116n7; divisions in, 5, 61, 62, 69, 100; essentialism in, 62–63, 109; history of, 14–16, 26–27; international, 72, 74–77, 79; Jewish women's involvement in, 5–8, 12, 15–19, 56, 61–79, 95, 99–113; Judaism as basis for, 2, 19, 24–25, 29, 54–57, 87; Judaism as compatible with, 18, 19, 32, 43–59, 85–88, 93–94, 97, 111–112; lesbian, 15, 16, 47–48, 68, 73, 104–105; lesbian separatists and, 11, 104, 106, 107; liberal, 11, 14–16, 26–30, 32, 33, 101, 103–104, 110, 111; Marxist, 15, 16, 105, 106, 110; men involved in, 11, 19, 80–94; radical, 11, 15, 16, 27, 30–33, 35, 99, 100, 104–105, 109–110; and secular Judaism, 45–59; some Jewish men's hostility to, 34–35, 100; specific issues and activities of, 11, 81. *See also* Consciousness-raising; Gender; Jewish-feminism; Jewishness; Otherness; Patriarchy

Feminists against Anti-Semitism, 76

Feminist standpoint theory, 126n17
Freud, Sigmund, 121n32
Friedan, Betty, 12, 14, 15, 130n6

Gail (research subject), 102–103
Gender: Conservative Judaism and equality of, 1–2, 16–17, 26, 30, 32, 123n3; as contested identity category, 4, 5; equality in, as liberal feminism goal, 15, 26–30, 32, 33, 110; inequality of, in traditional Judaism, 16–19, 21–24, 27, 28, 30–42, 97; inequality of, linked to other social stratifications, 11, 15, 59, 83; intersection of, with other identities, 5, 61, 70, 78–79, 97; Jewish-feminism as working for equality of, in Jewish institutions, 16–19, 21–42, 96, 103–104; major religions as legitimizing divisions by, 31–32, 42, 49, 57; as overlooked in research on Jewish identity, 6, 97. *See also* Feminism (second-wave); Gender studies; Masculinity; Patriarchy; Sexism
Gender studies, 11, 82, 120n24. *See also* Men's studies; Women's studies
Gerald (research subject), 92–93, 103
"Godwrestling," 124n9
Goodman, Saul, 44

Hagaddah, 47, 57
Haskalah movement, 44–45
Hebrew Bible, 21, 23, 24
Hebrew language: in interviews, 8; learning, 30, 34; love of, 33; skill in, 26
Hebrew school, 30, 92, 105
Heterosexuals: criticism of, 33, 62, 100, 104; among feminist research subjects, 7, 83, 99–100, 104, 105–106, 112
Holocaust, 6, 43, 48, 56, 68, 95; feelings associated with, 85, 92; survivors of, 89, 111
Humanistic Judaism, 14, 45–46, 105

Identities: American Jewish, and Israel, 75–79; changeability of, 10, 96–98; construction of Jewish masculine, 80–94; Freud's, 121n32; gender as overlooked in research on Jewish, 6, 97; intersection of gender with other, 5, 61, 70, 78–79, 97; invisibility of Jewish, in social activ-

ist groups, 62, 63–74, 79; loss of Jewish, 43; narratives of, 20, 51–52, 94, 96; national, 45, 121n32; negotiating and constructing complex and multiple, 2–4, 7, 11, 14, 20, 56, 58–59, 63, 71, 79, 94, 96; others' perception of one's, 60–61. *See also* Feminism (second wave); Intersectionality; Jewishness; Jews; Masculinity; Religion
Immigrants: assimilation as emphasis of Jewish, 63, 66–67, 90, 92; Jews as, 12, 14, 16, 45, 56, 87, 89, 92, 99, 109
Intersectionality, 5, 11, 61, 70, 97
Israel, 1, 14, 26, 35, 75–79, 102, 107, 125n24, 128n9

Jane (abortion service), 130n9
Janet (research subject), 25–26, 103–104
Jennifer (research subject), 38–40, 42, 52–53, 62, 72–74, 104
"Jewdar," 65
Jewish Enlightenment, 44–45
Jewish-feminism: discourse of congruence in, 19, 43, 51, 55, 57, 58–59, 93–94; among Orthodox Jews, 12; as oxymoron, 41–42; scholarship on, 17, 22–24, 26, 31, 34–36; as working for gender equality in Jewish institutions, 16–19, 21–42, 96, 103–104
"Jewish mothers," 9, 104
Jewishness: ambivalence about, 63, 77–79; asserting, 71–74; as contested identity category, 4, 11, 12–14; as cultural identity, 13, 38, 40, 43–50, 56, 58, 59, 79, 90, 100, 110; defined, 13, 95–96, 121n33; discourses of, 53–54; as ethnicity, 13, 44, 62, 65–66, 79, 96; as framework on the world, 54; older second-wave feminists' increasing identification with, 5–6, 25, 26, 30–31, 36, 64, 71, 74, 79, 101, 103–105, 107, 109–111; overlooked as contested category in women's studies, 5, 61–63, 70, 79, 97; personal styles associated with, 38, 73–74, 104; as race, 5–6, 13–14, 60–62, 70, 71; as religious identity, 13, 21–42, 45, 59, 65–67, 79, 95–96. *See also* Assimilation; Communities; Judaism; Otherness; Questioning; Social justice

Jewish Renewal, 14, 26, 124n10
Jewish studies, 17, 18, 24, 34, 65, 102, 127n1
Jews (American): Ashkenazi, 7, 13–14, 71, 106; and class, 14, 55, 61, 66–69, 88, 107; difficulties of defining, 13–14, 79, 95–96; as immigrants, 12, 14, 16, 45, 56, 63, 66–67, 87, 89, 92, 99, 109; origins of, in oppression, 6, 78–79; practicing, 7, 12–13, 21–42, 51, 95, 101, 109, 110, 112; radical movement involvement of women among, 11–12, 16–18, 35, 63, 99–104, 107, 110, 112; secular, 7, 12–13, 38–42, 44–59, 85, 92, 95, 102, 104, 106, 109, 110; as a utopian people, 55; as "white," 5–6, 13–14, 60–62, 70, 71. See also Anti-Semitism; Assimilation; Jewishness; Judaism; Persecution
Jill (research subject), 46, 47, 51, 64, 104–105
Judaism: as basis for feminism, 2, 19, 24–25, 29, 54–57, 87; belief in God not a requirement in, 46; cognitive dissonance between feminism and, 2, 10, 18, 19, 30–42, 44, 48–50, 59, 78, 91–92; as compatible with feminism, 18, 19, 32, 43–59, 85–88, 93–94, 97, 111–112; defined, 121n33; feminist reconstruction of, 16–19, 21–42, 91–92, 97; gender inequality in traditional, 16–19, 21–24, 27, 28, 30–42, 97; Jewish identity sometimes based on, 13, 21–42, 45, 59, 65–67, 79, 95–96; many Jews as not practicing, 7, 12–13, 38–42, 44–59, 92, 95, 102, 104, 106, 109, 110; as patriarchal religion, 18, 22, 30, 31–33, 36, 48, 49–50, 86, 90, 91–92, 103; practices of, 1, 8, 12, 19, 21–37, 47, 51, 52–53. See also Communities; Jewish-feminism; Jewishness; Questioning; Rabbis; Social justice; and entries for specific denominations

Kaddish, 39, 125n25
Kathie (research subject), 50, 53–54, 64, 66, 105
Kennedy, John F., 14

Labor movement and labor unions, 16, 58, 63, 99, 106, 121n29

Lebanon war, 78
Left, The, 13, 56, 64, 65–67, 77, 79, 102, 103, 105, 124n10. See also Anti–Vietnam War movement; Civil rights movement; Communism; SDS; Socialism
Lesbian(s): as critics of second-wave feminism, 5, 100; among feminist research subjects, 7, 25, 50, 58, 100, 101, 104–105, 107, 109, 110, 113; Jewish congregations for, 21–22, 25; study of, in women's studies, 62. See also Lesbian feminism
Lesbian feminism, 15, 16, 47–48, 68, 73, 104–105
Life history interviews, 4, 7–8, 10, 116n8. See also Biographical sketches of research subjects
Lisa (research subject), 47, 50, 55, 64, 77–78, 105–106

Makhloket. See Questioning
March on Washington, 110
Marginalization. See Otherness
Mark (research subject), 85–90, 92, 93, 106
Marx, Karl, 13
Marxist feminism, 15, 16, 105, 106, 110
Masculinity (construction of Jewish), 19, 50, 80–94
Men: hostility to feminism from, 34–35, 100; as privileged over women in Jewish families, 24, 30, 41–42, 110; profeminist, 11, 19, 80–94; research subjects' experiences with rabbinical, 34, 37, 39–40, 52, 107. See also Masculinity; Men's groups; Men's studies; Patriarchy; Rabbis; Violence against women
Men's groups (feminist), 11, 81, 111
Men's studies, 11, 101. See also Masculinity
Mental illness, 9–10, 21, 107, 109
Mexico City (Mexico), 75, 76
Miriam (research subject), 62, 72, 73, 106–107
Mitzvot, 23, 52, 53
Morality. See Social justice
Ms. Magazine, 100
Multiculturalism, 5, 6, 14, 61–63, 69–71, 79, 97. See also Ethnic studies
Music (women's), 11, 105, 112

Nancy (research subject), 107
Naomi (research subject), 34–35, 76, 107–108, 121n29
Natalie (research subject), 28, 108
National Conference on Jewish Women, 16
National identity, 45, 121n32
National Organization for Women (NOW), 11, 15; research subjects' involvement in, 29, 100, 101, 103, 108–111, 122n39
National Women's Studies Association (NWSA), 76
NOW. *See* National Organization for Women

Olivia (research subject), 71, 108–109
Oral histories. *See* Life history interviews
Orthodox Judaism, 51, 115n3; and gender inequality, 1–2, 17, 23, 24, 28–30, 41–42; and Jewish-feminists, 12, 121n30, 124n17; *mitzvot* in, 51–53; research subjects with, in family background, 12, 28, 29, 41–42, 54, 89, 99, 103, 107, 110; varieties of, 14. *See also* Ultra-Orthodox Judaism
Oslo (Norway), 76
Otherness (marginalization; feeling like an outsider): feeling of, among second-wave Jewish feminists in women's movement, 6, 19, 61–79, 95, 105, 106–107, 113; Jewish men as experiencing sense of, 19, 89, 92; of Jewish studies in the academy, 127n1; Jewish women's sense of, in traditional Judaism, 33, 37–42; Jews as experiencing racial, 13; of women and Jews relative to mainstream society, 19, 50, 51–52, 55–56, 58–59, 92. *See also* Anti-Semitism; Persecution
Outsider. *See* Otherness
Ozick, Cynthia, 38

Palestine, 76–78
Participant observation methods, 9–10
Passover, 47, 56
Patriarchy: elimination of, as radical feminism goal, 15, 30, 110; Judaism as rooted in, 18, 22, 30, 31–33, 36, 48, 49–50, 86, 90, 91–92, 103; as root cause of all oppressions, 109. *See also* Gender; Masculinity; Sexism

Persecution (of Jews), 6, 55, 56, 61, 68–69. *See also* Anti-Semitism; Holocaust; Otherness
Place of residence, and identity construction, 4, 116n9
Polygyny, 123n49
Posen Foundation, 45
Presidential Commission on the Status of Women, 14
"Profeminist," 127n1. *See also* Men: profeminist

Questioning (as Jewish tradition), 17–19, 25, 26, 51–52, 55–57, 83, 85, 90, 94

Rabbis: and construction of Jewish masculinity, 84; in history, 87, 123n49; power of, 40, 97; research subjects' exclusion from becoming, 28, 108; research subjects' experiences with female, 25, 31, 36; research subjects' experiences with male, 34, 37, 39–40, 52, 107; research subjects married to, 29, 111; women's ordination as, 16–18, 24, 27, 30, 35
Race: as division in feminist movement, 5, 61, 62, 69; and intersectionality, 5, 11, 70, 97; of Jews as contested notion, 5–6, 13–14, 60–62, 70, 71; in Marxist feminism, 105, 110; of research subjects, 83, 97. *See also* Racism
Rachel (research subject), 21–22, 25, 74, 109
Racism, 38, 54, 70, 75, 76. *See also* Civil rights movement
Randi (research subject), 38, 49–50, 58–59, 109–110
Rape. *See* Violence against women
Rebecca (research subject), 30–31, 33, 34, 76–77, 110
Reconstructionist Judaism, 14, 16, 30, 31, 102–103
"Red diaper" babies, 54, 57, 63, 99, 106, 112–113, 121n29. *See also* Communism
"Redlining," 67
Redstockings (radical feminist group), 100, 104
Reform Judaism, 14; gender equality in, 16–17, 30; research subjects' involve-

ment with, 29–31, 107, 108, 111; social justice emphasis in, 24–25, 52
Religion: Communism as form of, 57, 113; fundamentalism in, 42, 47; opposition to, 43, 46, 47–49, 54, 87, 99, 100, 106, 108, 110; patriarchal basis of major, 31–32, 42, 49; as regressive, 13, 64, 65–67, 106; women's studies' overlooking of, 5, 61–63, 70, 79, 97. *See also* Atheism among some Jews; Christianity; Judaism
Reproductive rights, 11, 32, 81, 105, 107, 111–112
Rhonda (research subject), 43–44, 54, 65–66, 68, 70, 78, 110, 121n29
Roosevelt, Eleanor, 14
Rosalyn (research subject), 29, 111
Rosh Hashanah, 47

Sam (research subject), 10, 88–93, 111
Sarah (research subject), 32–34, 71, 111–112
SDS (Students for a Democratic Society), 101, 109
Second-wave feminism. *See* Feminism (second-wave)
Secularism. *See* Jews (American): secular
Sexism: American, 85–86; childhood experiences of, in traditional Judaism, 37–42; of male rabbis, 34, 102–103, 107; opposition to, by men, 101; in social protest movements, 99, 100, 102, 106. *See also* Feminism (second wave); Gender; Otherness; Patriarchy
Sexual orientation, 5, 7, 11, 61, 70. *See also* Heterosexuals; Lesbian(s)
Shulas, 45
Socialism, 54, 63, 99, 102, 105, 107, 110, 121n29. *See also* Bund
Social justice: as key part of Judaism, 19, 29, 43, 45, 46, 51–59, 83, 85, 88, 91, 94, 95, 105, 111; not seen as a Jewish obligation by Orthodox Jews, 51, 52. *See also* Anti–Vietnam War movement; Civil rights movement; Feminism (second wave); *Tikkun olam*
Society of Humanistic Judaism, 45–46
Stereotypes: of Jewish men, 83–84, 89–94, 128n9; of Jewish women, 9, 73, 104
Steven (research subject), 69, 90–93, 112
Student protest movement, 43. *See also*

Anti–Vietnam War movement; Civil rights movement; SDS
Students for a Democratic Society (SDS), 101, 109
Suffrage movement, 15, 16

Talmud, 1–2, 23, 57, 116n5
Terry (research subject), 47–48, 50, 57–58, 73, 112–113
Theater (feminist), 11, 17, 51, 103, 104
Tikkun olam (repairing the world), 25, 51, 52–55
Torah. *See* Education (Jewish)

Ultra-Orthodox Judaism, 1–2, 35, 115n3
Unions. *See* Labor movement and labor unions
United Nations Decade for Women (Mexico City), 75, 76
United Nations International Conferences on Women, 75–77
United States: race and class as dividing lines in, 61; status of Jews in, 13, 14, 59, 61, 66–79, 101, 102, 109; on Zionism equals racism resolution, 75. *See also* Feminism (second-wave); WASP culture

Violence against women, 11, 81, 93–94, 101, 102, 108, 112; by Jewish men, 38, 87–88, 90, 91, 104; research subjects' personal experience with, 104. *See also* Battered women's shelters
Vorspan, Albert, 29

Wailing Wall (Western Wall), 1, 35, 125n24
WASP culture, 62, 73, 74, 83, 89
Whites (Jews seen as), 5–6, 13–14, 60–62, 70, 71
WITCH (Women's International Conspiracy from Hell), 104
Women of the Wall, 125n24
Women's International League for Peace and Justice, 78
Women's liberation movement. *See* Feminism (second-wave)
Women's music movement, 11, 105, 112
Women's Strike for Equality Day, 101, 130n6
Women's Strike for Peace, 78
Women's studies, 2, 11, 18, 102; confer-

ences on, 72–74, 76, 77; inclusion of,
in Jewish studies, 24; intersectionality
in, 5, 70; oppression emphasized in,
61, 69–70, 79; religion overlooked as
contested category in, 5, 61–63, 70, 79,
97; and second-wave feminism, 11, 18,
100, 104, 105, 108. *See also* Feminism
(second-wave): academic; Jewish-feminism: scholarship on

Women's Studies International, 77

Yiddishists, 45, 47, 50, 58, 105–106,
112–113, 121n29
Yiddish language, 8, 45, 106
Yom Kippur, 47

Zionism, 19, 45, 75–76

DINA PINSKY is an assistant
professor of sociology at Arcadia
University in Glenside, Pennsylvania.

The University of Illinois Press
is a founding member of the
Association of American University Presses.

Composed in 10/13 Sabon
by Jim Proefrock
at the University of Illinois Press
Designed by Kelly Gray
Manufactured by Thomson-Shore, Inc.
University of Illinois Press
1325 South Oak Street
Champaign, IL 61820-6903
www.press.uillinois.edu